WHEN
PEOPLE
THROW
STONES

WHEN PEOPLE THROW STONES

A Leader's Guide to Fielding Personal Criticism

BLAINE ALLEN

Kregel
Academic & Professional

When People Throw Stones: A Leader's Guide to Fielding Personal Criticism

© 2005 by Blaine Allen

Published by Kregel Publications, a division of Kregel, Inc., P.O. Box 2607, Grand Rapids, MI 49501.

Library of Congress Cataloging-in-Publication Data
Allen, Blaine.
    When people throw stones: a leader's guide to fielding personal criticism / by Blaine Allen.
        p. cm.
Includes bibliographical references.
    1. Interpersonal relationships—Religious aspects—
Christianity. 2. Conflict management—Religious
aspects—Christianity. 3. Criticism, Personal. 4. Fault-
finding. 5. Blame—Religious aspects—Christianity.
6. Forgiveness of sin. 7. Leadership—Religious aspects—
Christianity. I. Title.
BV4597.53.C58A45   2005
253'.2—dc22   2005002247

ISBN 0-8254-2014-8

Printed in the United States of America

05 06 07 08 09 / 5 4 3 2 1

CONTENTS

INTRODUCTION: A TERRORIST? 9

1. WHEN YOU CAN'T TAKE ANY MORE 13

2. WHEN YOU'VE DONE YOUR BEST 27

3. WHEN GOD DOESN'T DEFEND 45

4. WHEN YOUR CRITIC SPEAKS THE TRUTH 65

5. WHEN TO BLOW IT OFF 83

6. WHEN TO TAKE A STAND 97

7. WHEN SURVIVAL TECHNIQUES MAKE IT EASIER 113

8. WHEN PRIMED TO FIRE 129

9. WHEN AN EXPLOSION SEEMS INEVITABLE 143

10. WHEN YOU DON'T WANT TO FORGIVE 157

ENDNOTES 173

A TERRORIST?

No, not really. But in your less-than-better moments, you have thought that, have you not? They were so nice. So unassuming. So service oriented. And then boom! With words strapped to bombs, those whom you serve let it rip. Innuendo. Gossip. Criticized before others. An outright frontal attack. When the smoke clears, it feels as if your life, your family, and for sure your ministry, lie in a bloody ruin. You expect it from those who make no claim to know the Lord, but from those who say they are His followers?

In a rustic area not too far from where I live, the professionals call them "straight drops." No concrete vault. No plastic liner. Nothing but a poor man's pine box wrapped in glorified contact paper. After the reading of Scripture, the last prayer, and the family's final good-byes, grave diggers do what they are there for—drop the departed straight into the dirt.

Nobody wants to be "straight dropped." Bludgeoned with a verbal ax, thrown into a body bag, tossed into the dirt—nobody wants that. But many a pastor, staff member, missionary, teacher, administrator, parachurch worker, dedicated volunteer, have felt just that. Somebody was not pleased with their ministry, and did their critics ever let them know it!

Jonathan Swift, though from another century, speaks with eloquence as he describes the spirit behind words that chop:

A malignant deity, called Criticism. . . . At her right hand
sat Ignorance, her father and husband, blind with age; at
her left, Pride, her mother, dressing her up in scraps of
paper she herself had torn. There was Opinion, her sister,
light of foot, hoodwinked, and headstrong, yet giddy and
perpetually turning. About her played her children, Noise
and Impudence, Dullness and Vanity, Positiveness, Pedantry,
and Ill-Manners. The goddess herself had claws like a cat,
her head, and ears, and voice resembled those of an ass;
her teeth fallen out before, her eyes turned inward, as if she
also looked only upon herself; her diet was the overflowing
of her own gall.[1]

Maybe for you it's not so much the words as the stifling environ-
ment of displeasure. By the tone of voice and the demeanor behind
what is said, you know they are unhappy. You can hear it in the meet-
ings. You can sense it in the halls. You can just tell it, and it leaves you
in a pool of pain. In fact, you've heard through the grapevine that
you've become the target of tongues that zing words like bullets from
an automatic. All that's left at the yellow taped-off crime scene is a
chalk outline . . . of you. Straight dropped.

The word *dismiss* may even be whispered. It may be more than
whispered. You do not satisfy the expectations of those you serve.
You do not meet their needs. It's obvious they want a change, and
that change is not going to be them. Words fly. Fragments bury deep.
You feel disfigured. You wonder if others see your wounds. You wonder how much they have heard. Chop. Chop. Chop. What a harrow-
ing experience! Straight dropped.

And you are about to die. Die by giving up on others. Die by giving
up on ministry. And worst of all, die by giving up on the One who has
died for you. Words destroy people, and that's especially so in ministry. They can maul you to an emotional death. Is there life after that?
Is there ministry after that? If there is, how do you get it?

You could try anger. Vent your spleen. Do what Samson did: "Finding a fresh jawbone of a donkey, he grabbed it and struck down a
thousand men. Then Samson said, 'With a donkey's jawbone I have
made donkeys of them'" (Judg. 15:15–16). Because we naturally have

a low tolerance for those who find fault with us, we could reason that
our critic is, at best, the south end of a north-bound mule.

Taking very personally what was said about his daughter, a father
wrote:

> I have read your lousy review of Margaret's concert. I've come
> to the conclusion that you are "an eight ulcer man on four
> ulcer pay." . . . Some day I hope to meet you. When that
> happens you'll need a new nose, a lot of beefsteak for black
> eyes, and perhaps a supporter below.
>
> —HARRY S. TRUMAN[2]

You could go after your critic. You could try anger to revive your
emotional life, but all your anger will do is raze everything in sight—
including you.

You could kiss it off. But it's obvious you have not done that,
otherwise you wouldn't have picked up this book.

You could bite your tongue. But will that give you a new, more
livable world, and a fresh start? Or will it just drop you deeper into an
emotional grave? How do you get your life and ministry back when
those you serve make you hurt?

This is where criticism will make or break us. All responses are not
equal; each context has its own profile. But to survive, all responses
must be biblical. That is the "why" of this book: to help the ditched
climb out of an emotional grave, so as to live and continue to minister.

William Willimon shared:

> Last year a former student of mine at the Divinity School
> wrote of his struggles in his first parish. Despite his efforts to
> minister to these people, to serve them, to give them the
> kind of leadership they needed, they complained that he was
> not attentive enough, that he was not helpful enough to them.
>
> "But I've been going through weekly chemotherapy for
> my cancer," he said to them.
>
> "That's no excuse," they said. "You're the pastor."[3]

Sticks and stones may break my bones, but words will never hurt me.

We know better than that. They do hurt. They hurt us. They hurt our spouses. They hurt our children. They hurt our ministries. And the hurt can fester: resentment, bitterness, spite, rage. The adage is just simply not true. In fact, words can do more than hurt. Emotionally, words can kill. Life is no longer life. Ministry is no longer ministry.

Your critics may know the price of everything, but they likely do not know the value of you. The Father does. Others that love you do, too. Join me as we learn together how to make it *When People Throw Stones*.

Chapter 1

WHEN YOU CAN'T TAKE ANY MORE

I don't see how I can go on. I am so weary. I am so empty. And the critics just will not stop. They are on me like white on rice. The things I need to do, I just cannot do. Ministry needs . . . caring for my home . . . responsibilities beyond. The assault is just unbearable. Blaine, I just don't think I can handle it anymore.

It's been said widows fit one of two classes: the bereaved and the relieved. So it is with those who are widowed from a ministry. Either you'll really miss it, you hate to say good-bye; or you can hardly wait to shout, "Thank God, I am out!"

But very likely you are not ministry widowed. You are still there, still serving. And conceivably it's an impossible situation that right now is about to maul you to an emotional death. With a sharp eye for your faults and a blind eye for your strengths, your critics are dog determined to chew on you until there is nothing left to chew. Calvin Miller said, "Animosity cloaked in piety is a demon even if it sits in church praising the Creator."[1] No matter which way you turn or what direction you head, it's right there in your face: *"Hard pressed on every side . . . perplexed . . . persecuted . . . struck down."* What a way to live out your ministry days!

That was Paul. He felt everything a person could possibly feel—and then some—when under assault . . . and he survived. He shared the following:

> We are hard pressed on every side, but not crushed; per-
> plexed, but not in despair; persecuted, but not abandoned;
> struck down, but not destroyed.
>
> —2 CORINTHIANS 4:8–9

That's taking at high speed what you never thought you could take. That's thinking you are going to black out, but you don't. It's a fast nose dive, yet you walk away alive. Ministry for the servant is a nonstop test of who you are—in Christ. It's learning to adapt to the good times and the not-so-good times with the resources that are entrusted to every authentic follower of the Lord. It's understanding, as did Paul, how to live no matter what you face—"hard pressed on every side, but not crushed; perplexed, but not in despair; perse-cuted, but not abandoned; struck down, but not destroyed."

Now for the rest of his story:

> But we have this treasure in jars of clay to show that this all-
> surpassing power is from God and not from us. We are hard
> pressed on every side, but not crushed; perplexed, but not in
> despair; persecuted, but not abandoned; struck down, but not
> destroyed. We always carry around in our body the death of
> Jesus, so that the life of Jesus may also be revealed in our body.
> For we who are alive are always being given over to death for
> Jesus' sake, so that his life may be revealed in our mortal body.
>
> —2 CORINTHIANS 4:7–11

The following are some truths to embrace when you don't think you can take any more. You won't walk on water, but if you take them to heart, you will learn how to swim.

TRUTH: *You Cannot Handle Things*

On their way home from attending an Ash Wednesday service, little Johnny asked his mother, "Is it true, Mommy, that we are made of dust like the minister said tonight?"

"Yes, darling," his mother answered.

"And is it true that we go back to dust again when we die?"

"Yes, dear," his mother replied.

"Well, Mommy, when I said my prayers last night and looked under the bed, I saw someone who is either coming or going."[2]

Maybe that is you with your ministry—borderline dust, not sure whether you are coming or going, on the way to being swept, sucked up, and trashed in your critic's vacuum cleaner canister. If that is you, then you are close to taking your first significant step toward survival. You now have the opportunity to see things as they are: *You really are unable to cope with what others dish out; you really cannot handle things.*

Notice how Paul embraced this reality when he characterized himself along with his friends as "jars of clay" (2 Cor. 4:7). Not macho, not "got it all together." Not super-saint, not "suck up your guts no matter what." A clay pot. Brittle. Breakable. A clay pot that chips. A clay pot that cracks. A clay pot that, if ever compressed, would crumble. Paul's physical and emotional stamina (and that of his friends) was that of "jars of clay."

Are you sitting down? Good. Now for a dose of reality. You are not super-leader. You are not super-speaker. You are not super-pastor. You are not super-staff. You are not super-missionary. You are not super-volunteer. You are a pot. A breakable, brittle pot. A clay pot that chips. A clay pot that cracks. A clay pot that crumbles. You are nothing more than a jar of clay. Not even a super-pot. Just a pot.

Are you still sitting down? Good.

God meant for you to be that way.

> Can a mortal be more righteous than God?
>   Can a man be more pure than his Maker?
> If God places no trust in his servants,
>   if he charges his angels with error,
> how much more those who live in houses of clay,
>   whose foundations are in the dust,
>   who are crushed more readily than a moth!
>   —JOB 4:17-19

Show me, O Lord, my life's end
and the number of my days;
let me know how fleeting is my life.

You have made my days a mere handbreadth;
the span of my years is as nothing before you.
Each man's life is but a breath.   *Selah*

Man is a mere phantom as he goes to and fro:
He bustles about, but only in vain;
he heaps up wealth, not knowing who will get it.

—PSALM 39:4–6

Remember how fleeting is my life.
For what futility you have created all men!

What man can live and not see death,
or save himself from the power of the grave?

Selah

—PSALM 89:47–48

You turn men back to dust,
saying, "Return to dust, O sons of men."

For a thousand years in your sight
are like a day that has just gone by,
or like a watch in the night.

You sweep men away in the sleep of death;
they are like the new grass of the morning—

though in the morning it springs up new,
by evening it is dry and withered.

—PSALM 90:3–6

For my days vanish like smoke.

—PSALM 102:3A

O LORD, what is man that you care for him,
the son of man that you think of him?

Man is like a breath;
his days are like a fleeting shadow.

—PSALM 144:3-4

All men are like grass,
and all their glory is like the flowers of the field.

The grass withers and the flowers fall,
because the breath of the LORD blows on them.

—ISAIAH 40:6B-7A

Now listen, you who say, "Today or tomorrow we will go to this or that city, spend a year there, carry on business and make money." Why, you do not even know what will happen tomorrow. What is your life? You are a mist that appears for a little while and then vanishes.

—JAMES 4:13-14

The stamina of a moth. A breath. Smoke. A phantom. Dust. A shadow. Grass that withers. Flowers that drop off. Mist that evaporates. A "jar of clay." Not exactly nerves of steel. Friend, God meant for you not to be able to handle it. That's reality. That's the way things really, really are. That's me. That's you.

And because that is both of us, when we are faced with what we cannot face, then we eye an opportunity to take that first significant step toward survival—accepting from our heart of hearts that God never intended for us to be able to "super-pot" our way through ministry. The feeling of helplessness you experience is from Him. It's God's in-your-face way of saying, "I know you can't. Now *you* need to know you can't. You are just a breakable, brittle jar of clay."

Surprised by that sense of inner helplessness? Don't be. Don't get blown away by that feeling you just cannot "hack it" any more. Pots are supposed to feel that. If you don't realize that your sense of vulnerability is a gift from God, you will get caught off guard and do something stupid. Neither you nor I will learn to cope God's way until we see ourselves God's way—as fragile jars of clay.

> *Lord, I hate this feeling. I want to run from this feeling. Helplessness. Vulnerability . . . profound inner weakness . . . none of it, Lord, do I want. But Lord, You did not make me superman. Not even super-pot. Just a jar of clay that will break. And I receive the way I've been made from You. Help me not to despise my weakness. Help me not to run from my sense of frailty. Thank You for using this situation to help me see myself as I really am: one who cannot handle things.*

TRUTH: *Anticipate That God Will Handle Things*

Friend, your feebleness is not fatal. That sick, sinking feeling is not final. If you belong to the Lord and understand His purpose when overwhelmed by "too much," you will not drown. Just the opposite: You've made a second significant step toward emotional survival when your critic's words kill. Motivated by a tremendous sense of felt-need, you look to Another for help. That is Paul's point in 2 Corinthians 4:7 when he calls us "jars of clay."

God's purpose in that helpless feeling is not to sit back and watch you gulp for emotional air before you drown. It's to communicate to you that as a child of the King, you have divine resources. Any demand made upon you is a demand made upon your God.

That's the treasure in the jars of clay—an all-surpassing power. It's God's power, an omnipotence that is certainly able to give us strength through whatever comes. This power is not just to compensate for pots. It transcends that reality. This is the all-surpassing power that causes others to wonder, "How can he take what he takes? I couldn't do that!" That's the paradox: You can't take it. There's no way you can handle it. You already should have drowned.

You are still afloat because you've learned to stop despising that helpless feeling. You see it as God's "attention grabber" to remind you that "When I can't, He can." Moment by moment, you believe that He will, for any demand made upon you is a demand made upon Him.

It's that divine treasure stashed down in your spiritual guts, a treasure received the moment you trusted Christ as your Savior.

> For God, who said, "Let light shine out of darkness," made his light shine in our hearts to give us the light of the knowledge of the glory of God in the face of Christ. But we have this treasure in jars of clay to show that this all-surpassing power is from God and not from us.
>
> —2 CORINTHIANS 4:6–7

We used to live in Chicago, just five minutes from O'Hare International Airport. For my departing flights I was always at the gate in plenty of time. For other people's flights, especially to meet an arriving passenger (before post-9/11 security restrictions), I ran late more than once. And since O'Hare has forever-and-ever tunnels to the main terminals and forever-and-ever concourses to the gates, a little late in the parking garage is a big late by the time you get to the gate—until I discovered the genius of moving sidewalks. These horizontal conveyor belts in major airports allow you to do what you never thought you could. If you walk while that sidewalk moves, you can cover ground in record time. Keep a good stride on moving sidewalks, and you will get to your gate super fast. As you do it, the moving sidewalk does it.

Hard pressed in ministry? Perplexed in ministry? Persecuted in ministry? Struck down in ministry? As you do it—continue to live in a way that honors the Lord, doing those things that you just did not think you could do—God does it.

> We are hard pressed on every side, but not crushed; perplexed, but not in despair; persecuted, but not abandoned; struck down, but not destroyed.
>
> —2 CORINTHIANS 4:8–9

Hard pressed on every side is a phrase that in the original language describes that feeling of being boxed in. You can't say, "Okay, enough of this problem, I'm out of here." There is no "out of here." There is no walking away. You are converged on from every angle. It's lockdown time, and the prisoner is you.

Perplexed is that feeling of not knowing what's going on. And in the context of ministry, that may include confusion over whether those you serve *want* you to serve them—even marginally serve them. You thought they were your fans, you thought they had accepted you. Then "whap" . . . right in the side. You are confused about the present and unsure about the future, although you've tried to be and do what God wants.

Persecuted means you get pursued with a vengeance. In a hypercritical context, it means you did not do it and you get nailed. You did do it and it was right that you did do it, and you get nailed. You explain why you did do what you did do and you get nailed. Pursued with a vengeance. Verbal hots poured down your neck, even though you believed that your choices honored the Lord. Persecuted.

Struck down is a chilling phrase, a "Where's God?" phrase. In terms of ministry, this is when it looks like God has turned His back on you, walked away, and thrown away your key of opportunity to enjoy any semblance of a blessed life ever again. You are dead meat.

- "You don't meet our needs."
- "You are not what we want."
- "It's time for you to go."
- "It's time for us to make sure that you do go."

Struck down—a bone-chilling phrase. Yet, friend, if you do as Paul, you will survive. That means you value the treasure within and expect that treasure to be the difference for you, no matter what you face. As you do it—continue to live in a way that honors the Lord, doing those things that you just did not think you could do—God does it.

Pressure on the outside? A greater pressure on the inside.

Unbelievable force on the surface? An even greater unbelievable force at the center.

A push to put you over the edge? A harder pull to keep you from the edge.

> Fear not, for I am with you;
> Be not dismayed, for I am your God.

I will strengthen you,
Yes, I will help you,
I will uphold you with My righteous right hand.

—ISAIAH 41:10 NKJV

We do not want you to be uninformed, brothers, about the hardships we suffered in the province of Asia. We were under great pressure, far beyond our ability to endure, so that we despaired even of life. Indeed, in our hearts we felt the sentence of death. But this happened that we might not rely on ourselves but on God, who raises the dead. He has delivered us from such a deadly peril, and he will deliver us. On him we have set our hope that he will continue to deliver us.

—2 CORINTHIANS 1:8–10

Not that we are sufficient of ourselves to think of anything as being from ourselves, but our sufficiency is from God.

—2 CORINTHIANS 3:5 NKJV

I have been crucified with Christ; it is no longer I who live, but Christ lives in me; and the life which I now live in the flesh I live by faith in the Son of God, who loved me and gave Himself for me.

—GALATIANS 2:20 NKJV

I can do all things through Christ who strengthens me.

—PHILIPPIANS 4:13 NKJV

Don't despise difficult times. If you know the Lord, it's the perfect opportunity for God to be God in you, to show you that no matter what takes place on the outside, He will take care of you on the inside. If you are taken care of on the inside, by His grace you can take care of what needs to be done on the outside. As you do it, He does it.

Lord, I see it in the Word, but I'm still having a hard time believing it. Help my unbelief. I know I am a clay pot. I know I am fractured

and am close to getting crushed. But You are my treasure within,
Your all-surpassing power. I am asking You to do for me what You
have done for Paul and others when hard pressed on every side,
perplexed, persecuted, struck down: Be Yourself, moment by moment,
in me. Thank You.

NOW WHAT?

Granted, when super-stressed in ministry, this is not an approach that you hear much about. Next to today's "how-to" strategies for serving, it really seems foolish and simplistic, an outlook that does not grapple realistically with the issues faced.

It's similar to the instance in Matthew 12:13 when Jesus told the man with the shriveled hand, "Stretch out your hand." What kind of simplistic approach was that? If the man could stretch out his hand, he already would have stretched out his hand. So unrealistic. So pie in the sky. Then "he stretched it out and it was completely restored, just as sound as the other" (v. 13b).

Or what about in Mark 2:11 when Jesus said to the paralytic, who was possibly even a quadriplegic, "I tell you, get up, take your mat and go home." What kind of an off-the-wall remark was that? Talk about an approach that does not grapple with the issues. If the man could get up, he would have gotten up a long time ago. So out of touch. So impractical. Yet verse 12 states: "He got up, took his mat and walked out in full view of them all. This amazed everyone and they praised God, saying, 'We have never seen anything like this!'"

What God commands, God empowers. When you command your TV remote, you see to it the television is empowered; you make sure it's plugged into some electricity. What we command when it comes to a TV, we empower.

What God commands in anyone, anything, any setting, God empowers. And as a servant, since God commands you to be diligent in all you do, you can.[3] You can lead. You can prepare so you have something of significance to say when it is time to speak. You can give it your all when working with others. You can give it your all when working alone. You can minister among your critics, carrying out your God-assigned responsibilities in a way that honors the Lord. Diligence. You can.

The same is true with faithfulness. Since God commands you to be faithful, you can.[1] You can be faithful with your time. You can be faithful with your emotions. You can be faithful with the gospel. You can be faithful as an example to others to motivate them to good deeds. You can be faithful and so encourage the weak and cheer the strong. You can be faithful at home so your spouse and children are built up. Faithfulness. You can.

Likewise with love. Since God commands you to love your neighbors, you can.[5] You can love them with your care. You can love them with your ear. You can love them with your words. You can love them if they are on your team. You can love them if they are not. You can love them if they are up in the stands booing your every call. Love. You can.

Friend, what God commands, God empowers. As you do it—even though you don't feel like doing it—God does it.

> But we have this treasure in jars of clay to show that this all-surpassing power is from God and not from us. . . . We always carry around in our body the death of Jesus, so that the life of Jesus may also be revealed in our body. For we who are alive are always being given over to death for Jesus' sake, so that his life may be revealed in our mortal body.
>
> —2 CORINTHIANS 4:7-11

The treasure—that all-surpassing power—is the very life of Jesus. When you are put in a "death situation" for Jesus' sake, His life is released through you at that moment. And within the context of ministry, a death situation includes the unscrupulous, thoughtless tongue of another who feels an unusual freedom to carve you up for no wrong that you have done. Your life in all that you face becomes Christ's life in all that you face.

It's there in these verses. When you face tough times, God reveals in your body the very life of the Son of God. What you read in the Bible about His peace, His composure, His graciousness, His ability to face opposition, His love, His willingness to forgive, His endurance—that's what God releases in you. Dallas Willard, professor of philosophy at the University of Southern California, lecturer and writer on philosophy and religion, states:

As Paul says to the Corinthians, "We have this treasure in earthen vessels." You cannot avoid having a vessel. The problem comes when you mistake the vessel for the treasure, for the treasure is the life and power of Jesus Christ. I am sorry to say, but too much of what we call "Christian" is not a manifestation of the supernatural life of God in our souls. Too much of what we call "Christian" is really just human.[6]

Dear one, when you hurt, "just human" is not going to do it. When hard pressed from all sides, you will collapse. When perplexed, you will despair. When persecuted, you will feel abandoned. When struck down, you will look like Humpty Dumpty after his great fall. "Just human" will not do it. To survive, there must be the "manifestation of the supernatural life of God in our souls."

Comparing the relationship to the "one flesh" of marriage, Paul writes in 1 Corinthians 6:17, "he who unites himself with the Lord is one with him in spirit." Remember that we are two-faceted—a visible material part (the body) and an invisible immaterial part (the soul and spirit, a part that includes the mind, the emotions, the heart). In that invisible immaterial part, before you were saved, there was *just you*. When you trusted Christ as your Savior—"united yourself to the Lord"—something changed. You did not feel it, but in that invisible immaterial part there was no longer *just you*. There's now *you and Christ*. His invisible immaterial part and your invisible immaterial part are now one in spirit in the same body.

You don't become a spiritual glowworm. You certainly don't become deity. And for sure, God doesn't become you. But now when you think about yourself, you need to understand that on the outside is a body, and on the inside are *you and Him*.

That is why any demand made upon you is a demand made upon Him. Any pressure applied to you is pressure applied to Him. Any "in-your-face" challenge directed toward you is an "in-your-face" challenge taken up by Him.

I have a lamp in a room at our house. It has a shade and a bulb. But when I click the switch, nothing. I have another lamp in the same room. It has a shade and a bulb. When I click the switch, there's light.

I can read by it, study by it, enjoy the presence of others by it. The difference? The live lamp is united to all the resources of my local electric company at the outlet on my wall, while the other's plug is lying on the floor. The live lamp has become one in spirit with the electricity of Four County Electric Cooperative, so that any demand made upon that lamp when the switch is clicked is a demand made upon Four County Electric.

Do you understand? Do you believe . . . really believe? Are you a person of faith with a "right now" trusting faith? If you are "given over to death" in your ministry "for Jesus' sake"—not for your own selfish, sinful sake—the supernatural current will flow. You won't feel some infusion of His presence. It's very likely that when you tell Him "I can't handle things, but I know You can," you won't feel a thing.

There are no advances. Just as your next breath is not an up-front allowance on oxygen for the rest of the day, your next spiritual breath is not spiritual oxygen for the rest of your ministry stress—only enough spiritual air to do what you need to do in that spiritual breath.

But because you are *one with Him in spirit,* His life will flow through you. Demands made on you are demands made upon Him, no matter how many times your switch gets clicked.

Do you understand? Do you believe? Do you really believe?

When you push your grocery cart to the car, you leave the store checkout counter with bags and bags of food. You head for the door, and you know it's closed. But you still push that buggy. You have to get your groceries out to the parking lot where your car is. And though the door is closed, you don't push that buggy out of despair. You push that buggy in hope. You really believe that when that door needs to open, it will open—automatic electric doors just do—and with confidence you press ahead.

Friend, that's what this chapter is about. It's not a denial that practical things such as counseling and mediation may need to be done in response to the criticism within your ministry. But it is saying that those things are meaningless and ultimately will do no good if you haven't made a commitment to keep pushing your buggy. If you learn to push your buggy in faith, even if a door is shut tight in front of you—"I can't"—you will discover that you can and can as long as God wants you to. An inadequate you. A more than adequate God.

That's what serving God is about. That's what the Christian life is about. That's why I know you can make it.

.

Chapter 2

WHEN YOU'VE DONE YOUR BEST

Every Monday morning by 7 A.M. I do it. Sometimes with an extra bag, occasionally with two. But most of the time it's just my gray container on wheels; out to the curb my trash bin goes. A week's worth of processed paper and food, and I'm finished with it. What once was good, the family never wants to see again. We are done with it. It's garbage.

Could it be? Is that really you sitting out on the curb waiting to be hauled off? You thought you had value to those you serve, but now it's Monday morning. What was said was so jagged and cut so deep. Maybe it was one of those heart-to-heart talks. Maybe it was said on the fly. Maybe it has been said and said again in different ways.

However it was said, the message is clear: You are to blame. You are the reason things are the way things are. By the time you had caught wind of it, the wind was gale force, strong enough to plaster your soul to the wall. It has been said that ministry is never as good as it seems; nor is it as bad. But this is bad.

You know you are not one of the "greats" from your people's past, but you thought they liked you the way you are. You thought they accepted you for who you are, with your abilities, personality, and temperament. Forget that. The differences between you and other leaders are now differences used against you.

"You know, our last pastor would have handled this differently."

"We used to have dynamic leadership around here."

"Wow, I would give anything to have *him* back on staff."

You wonder: "Am I wired wrong for ministry?" You are the first to admit that your spiritual gifts are less than spectacular, but they seemed a match for the setting. Others thought that they were a match. Even your critics thought it.

What changed?

"You just don't meet our needs."

"When that guest speaker spoke, we really felt like God was speaking."

"You simply are not effective."

Now add to the mix those who once were fans but who now sit on their hands. Sometimes silence is the most painful criticism of all. Whether with or without words, you feel trashed until you wonder: "Am I really that inept at doing what needs to be done?"

Could it be? Is that really you sitting out on the curb? Are you waiting for the truck to take you to the dump?

If that is you out on the curb, there's only one word for it: *rejection.*

"You have a very rare and extremely contagious condition," the doctor told his patient. "We're going to put you in an isolation unit where you'll be on a diet of pancakes and pizza."

"Will pancakes and pizza cure my condition?"

"No," replied the doctor. "They're the only things we can slip under the door."

Rejection. Plain, in-your-face rejection. Not just being criticized; even groundless criticism is not necessarily rejection. After all, those words may have been ignorant words, an isolated complaint, or hormones that just got the best of a person whose talk on another day, with a cooler head, would have sounded like anything but rejection. Words that strike us the wrong way are not always a non-refundable one-way ticket to the dump.

On the other hand, rejection does happen. Elders and deacons reject their pastors. Senior pastors reject staff members; ministry directors reject volunteers; congregations reject leaders; missionaries or parachurch workers reject one another.

It does happen. Good ministry partnerships are not perfect ministry partnerships. Good ministry partnerships are relationships that can ignore stubborn differences. Those that are less than good cannot. Differences reign. And when they reign, ministry is tough. You are a pebble in another's shoe. Not only are you not appreciated, you feel like you are not wanted. In fact, you may know you are not wanted.

It's not that you have been a model servant. You know better than that. It's not that you haven't contributed to the tension. You know better than that. But your critic—likely critics—have bagged you and rolled you to the curb, and it hurts. No longer is your presence valued. No longer are your thoughts wanted. You wait, emotionally stripped and all alone.

Question: What will it take to keep you off the garbage truck?

WHAT IT TOOK FOR ANOTHER

Mary, the sister of Lazarus and Martha, knew what it was to be wheeled out to the curb.

> While [Jesus] was in Bethany, reclining at the table in the home of a man known as Simon the Leper, a woman came with an alabaster jar of very expensive perfume, made of pure nard. She broke the jar and poured the perfume on his head. Some of those present were saying indignantly to one another, "Why this waste of perfume? It could have been sold for more than a year's wages and the money given to the poor." And they rebuked her harshly.
>
> —MARK 14:3–5

Bam! Right in the face. The word *harshly* comes from a term that means "to snort with anger." This is a stern, "drop-dead" tongue-lashing. It's a scolding of the worst sort. From parallel accounts in the Gospels we know that the uproar started with Judas.[1] To mask his greed with a "heart for the poor," the crook tore the woman apart.

And the others? Good people often get sucked into a tornado of criticism generated by only a few. "A stupid thing to do"—that's what Judas and others told Mary. They did it before her peers, before her relatives, before the One she wanted to please more than anyone

else. This was humiliation at its worst. Mary was shamed without any
chance for a defense.

The scene was a dinner in honor of the Lord at Simon the Leper's
house. And Mary interrupted it. No invitation. No "May I?" No "Please
excuse me, but . . ." She just arrived unannounced and did it.

But they took care of her. "She won't pull that stunt again. . . .
Hey, Peter, pass the potatoes." Bagged up like garbage, Mary was on
the way to the curb. Then the Lord spoke:

> "Leave her alone," said Jesus. "Why are you bothering her?
> She has done a beautiful thing to me. The poor you will al-
> ways have with you, and you can help them any time you
> want. But you will not always have me. She did what she could.
> She poured perfume on my body beforehand to prepare for
> my burial. I tell you the truth, wherever the gospel is preached
> throughout the world, what she has done will also be told, in
> memory of her."
>
> —MARK 14:6–9

Monday, 7:00 A.M., and there was no getting on the garbage truck;
no staying in the garbage can. Jesus' words energized Mary to handle
the harshest of criticism. It was the difference between life and the
dump. If you are sitting out on the curb, His words can also make the
difference for you.

FOR HIM

A few rules of the air that most pilots take to heart:

- Every takeoff is optional. Every landing is mandatory.
- It's always better to be down here wishing you were up there
  than up there wishing you were down here.
- Never let an aircraft take you somewhere your brain didn't get
  to five minutes earlier.
- The three most useless things to a pilot are the altitude above
  you, the runway behind you, and a tenth of a second ago.

While she was hurtling toward earth, Mary probably would have agreed. Her good deed was optional, not mandatory, but now it could not be undone. There was no getting back to where she had been before takeoff. "Why did I do this? I thought it was appropriate. I meant it to be for the Lord. Does He think the same? Did I embarrass Him before all these people, especially the men? I didn't mean to. I really do care for the poor. If only I had not let my emotions take me where my brain had not gone."

Misgivings. Doubts. It's not hard to imagine Mary's insides heaving. The dear lady was in a fast melt. Sometimes those kinds of painful questions are good. They force us to evaluate our choices—especially when we are under the fire of criticism. But when criticism is vicious, when it blindsides and leaves us in a nosedive, we need a stable horizon first. We need some spiritual point of reference, a grid to graph ourselves against so that we can step back to find out how things really are.

Mary found out the way things really were. When the Lord confronted her critics, was she ever glad that she had done what she did! "Why are you bothering her? She has done a beautiful thing to me" (Mark 14:6).

Have you been ripped up? Do you wish you could undo what looked like the right thing to do for God? Here's your stable reference point. Would the Lord look at the thing or things for which you were criticized and say that it was "beautiful" (the word means "choice, excellent, an intrinsically good effort") and done for Him?

Few things are quite as pure as Mary's act of devotion. You may not have been thinking, "This is for the Lord," when you did something. Nevertheless, whether at a job, in the church community, or at home, God calls all His children to live out Colossians 3:23–24: "Whatever you do, work at it with all your heart, as working for the Lord, not for men, since you know that you will receive an inheritance from the Lord as a reward. It is the Lord Christ you are serving." Has that been you?

In ministering to others, did you do it with all your heart? You were not negligent. You were not treating those you serve like last week's leftovers. You considered what you did to be significant because you knew intuitively what made it important was its importance to the Lord. Was that what you meant by your behavior, a behavior that you are now vilified for? Did you do it for Him?

If it was something you should not have done, the answer is *no*. If it was something you should have done but did not do, the answer is *no*. Ditto for what you said or didn't say. If you botched it, then admit that you botched it, and by the grace of God, do better next time.

But, assuming your behavior was not uncalled for, did you do what you are hosed down for as a beautiful thing for the Lord? The New King James Version translates our Lord's assessment of Mary's conduct: "She has done a good work for Me" (Mark 14:6). The New American Standard has it, "She has done a good deed to Me." Paul tells us in Philippians 2:13 that "it is God who works in you to will and to act according to his good purpose." In the believer's life, all good deeds are an outworking of God's in-working through His child's life. Thus, when an authentic servant chooses to do what is beautiful and good for those he serves, it is really something beautiful and good done by Him. And if it is done by Him, it is certainly acceptable to Him. And since all good deeds that are generated by our God are designed for His glory, all good and beautiful things done for those you minister to are good and beautiful things done for Him.[2]

Is that what you are taking heat over—a good deed done for others that in reality was a good deed done for the Lord? What you did and are now criticized for—whether just one particular thing or an array of things—was it beautiful, done for Him? That doesn't mean the deed was executed flawlessly. What makes it a beautiful thing done for the Lord is:

- the importance you gave to God's Word;
- your degree of preparation before you spoke;
- the integrity with which you spoke;
- your management of time;
- your care for those you serve;
- your identification with their needs;
- the way you challenged them to reach out;
- the sensitivity with which you introduced significant change;
- the grace with which you said "no";
- your conduct in administration;

- your desire to find better approaches to old problems;
- your respect for those who are older;
- your respect for those who are younger;
- your respect for authority;
- your honoring of traditions;
- your openness to new ideas;
- your leadership attitude;
- how you treated those who differed with you.

So, evaluate: Was it a good deed for those you serve that in reality was a good deed to the Lord, and you got nailed for it? Was it a beautiful thing, done for Him? Peter says, "Live such good lives among the pagans that, though they accuse you of doing wrong, they may see your good deeds and glorify God on the day he visits us" (1 Peter 2:12). Though your critic may not be a pagan (although the possibility may have crossed your mind!), have you as a servant of the Lord been living that "good life"? We are not talking about intentions. You and I can have the greatest of intentions in ministry and still fall short of living that "good life" that blesses others with good and beautiful actions.

Researchers in human behavior decided to find out whether people who trained for vocational ministry at seminaries are Good Samaritans. William McRae writes:

> They met individually with 40 of the ministerial students under the pretense of doing a study on careers in the church. Each student was instructed to walk to a nearby building to dictate an impromptu talk into a tape recorder there. Some were told to talk on the Good Samaritan parable, others on their career concerns. Meanwhile, the researchers planted an actor along the path who, as a seminarian approached, groaned and slumped to the ground. More than half the students walked right on by, reported the researchers in Human Behavior. "Some, who were planning their dissertation on the Good Samaritan, literally stepped over the slumped body as they hurried along."[3]

We are not talking about intentions. The smallest good deed is eternally better than the greatest feelings. We are talking about actually doing good and beautiful things for those you serve, which means those things were really done for the Lord.

Is that what you did and it has blown up in your face?

The more objectively you can look back and answer questions like these truthfully in the affirmative, the more likely you did as Mary did. You probably were not a perfect Mary. You probably were not even consciously a Mary. What the Lord wants is the same kind of spirit as Mary. Though you could not see Him, your words and actions gave to the Lord the same kind of gift she gave to the Lord. You gave yourself.

If in these things your heart does not condemn you, then take it as a witness of His Spirit; as far as you know this side of the judgment seat, you, too, poured out what you had *for Him*.

ACCORDING TO PLAN

Samuel Clemens reportedly said, "The good Lord didn't create anything without a purpose, but the fly comes close."

To Mary's critics, her perfume and what she did with it came even closer. "What a waste! What an unbelievable waste!"

But her act had historic purpose. It wasn't the price that set it apart—almost a year's wages for a "blue collar" worker. Neither was it the fragrance, a rare spice imported from northern India. The significance lay in what the gift was to be used for. In God's economy, this gift was marked to anoint the One who would bear Mary's sin. John records in his parallel account that the Lord said, "Leave her alone . . . . It was intended that she should save this perfume for the day of my burial" (John 12:7).

She could have used it for Lazarus, her brother, who had died just a little earlier. It would have been the customary thing to do. Fragrance such as this was often used in the burial of a loved one. But Mary did not. In the providence of God, it was planned by heaven that the flask was not to be used until a given time at a given place by a given person. It fulfilled a divine design for the Lord.

So it was done. Mary did what she was supposed to do with that alabaster vial of pure nard. It was intended that she should foreshadow with this perfume the Lord's burial.

Likely Mary did not realize when this most rare treasure first became hers that it was meant for Him. She did not understand when she pulled it out and unwrapped it at home that it had always been meant for Him. She had no idea as she cradled it on the way to Simon's house that she was moving according to plan. There were no voices, no visions. Mary simply followed a desire that was welling up from within to take what was very precious to her and worship the Lord Jesus with it.

She did not know the desire came from the Spirit, but it did. No accident. No afterthought. From God's perspective, nothing had been left to chance. On that particular day, before all those men, she was doing with her gift what God wanted her to do. Mary's critics raked her over the coals for an act from the Lord!

Ask yourself, Did you do what you were supposed to do because God wanted you to? Maybe you didn't realize it at the time, but how does it look with 20/20 hindsight? Do you see any clues of God's hand with you in what you did? Though criticized, maybe even harshly, do you detect any evidence of His will lived out by you?

No servant of the Lord has a greater ministry than that to his family. No criticism hurts worse than that which comes from home.

Sam and Jill had just moved to a new ministry.[4] They had prayed and prayed for a situation in which Sam could financially support the family and Jill could stay at home with their children. This was it. But no sooner had the movers departed than Jill turned shredder:

- You are too unspiritual to recognize that this is not God's will for us.
- You are just in it for the money.
- You've wrecked our future.
- If you loved me, you would go back.
- The reason God spoke to me that this move was wrong and not to you is because you are not one of His children.

Sam was stunned. Outside of her unusual quietness during the cross-country move, he had no hint that his wife was ready to blow.

But once she did, the lava flowed. Week after week it flowed. In serving others through his new position, Sam knew that home was where he was to serve first. And it was there that he seemed to have failed. Had he led his family wrong? Was his new ministry outside God's will? Was the fierce criticism right on?

Mary had one advantage in that the Lord was there to vocally give heaven's slant on the matter for all to hear. Not so for Sam. Instead, several months after he arrived, Sam was pouring his heart out to me, a local pastor.

We first talked about the obvious need for marriage counseling for both him and Jill. A crisis like this doesn't drop in totally "detached" from the past. Another set of problems was driving the critical response. But before we identified them, Sam needed immediate help. Was He doing what God wanted him to do? Was his family where God wanted them to be? Had he led his family out of God's will?

I prayed that God would give us wisdom in our discussions and then wrote down some of Jill's more brutal charges. That helped Sam to look back with a better eye over the whole episode.

Was he saved? Jill claimed he was not. I asked, "Sam, if you were to die and God asked you 'Why should I let you into my heaven?' What would you say?" Sam did not hesitate: "I would answer, 'I don't deserve to be in heaven except for what Jesus did for me. He died on the cross, paying in full the penalty for my sin, and in repentance I have placed my trust in Him and Him alone as my risen Savior and Lord.'"

The answers don't get any better than that.

Maybe Jill was being vindictive, engaging her mouth before she engaged her mind. We could at least record that she was wrong on that one. Sam knew he belonged to the Lord. I jotted it down.

Was he too unspiritual to recognize God's will? Possibly, but when questioned about his walk with the Lord over the previous twelve months, Sam had been more consistent in his quiet times than ever before. Pressed on moral issues and character issues, Sam could honestly say that he had been obedient. He had sought godly advice from others about the move. Jill had given every indication before the movers came that she too believed this was what God wanted. If there had not been agreement, Sam would not have moved.

Sam was no spiritual giant, but after we talked, he could look back and say he was in fellowship with the Lord when the decision was made. I jotted it down.

Was he in it for the money or out to wreck the family's future? Certainly money was a big part of it, but Sam had passed on better paying offers because of his family's emotional needs. Money itself did not tug at him; the money he was making was intended to take care of the family. Sam wanted to give Jill the opportunity to stay home. No, he was not in it for the money, and he certainly was not out to wreck his family, especially the children, who meant everything to him. I jotted it down.

Was this move proof that he did not love Jill? Jill wanted to go back and she expected Sam to do whatever it took to take her and the family back. When I read from Ephesians how the husband is to love his wife as Christ loved the church, Sam knew he loved Jill. Certainly his love was not up to the standard of Jesus Christ. With Christ as the model, he knew he needed to continue to work at sacrificial love. But he loved Jill. Sometimes in their marriage she was not easy to love, but he loved her. When she had done other "unexpected" things, he had hung tough with her. He tried to work with her this time. Though Jill had turned supercritical, Sam knew he still loved her. I jotted it down.

We both looked at the legal pad. The criticism was coming from the one he was to serve the most, his wife, but Sam was where he was, doing what he had moved to do, because God meant it to be so. If heaven had planned that for him as the God-assigned head of the family, then God had planned it to be so for his wife and children, too.

There was a sense of relief. Big relief. Though things would be tough with Jill, her words could not dictate God's perspective to him. He was going to have to do what harshly criticized people sometimes must do: develop the heart of the Savior and the hide of a rhinoceros. Indications were that Sam was acting according to plan. "Leave him alone . . . . It was intended that he serve Me this way."

Friend, with 20/20 hindsight, learn to "jot it down." If lava is getting spewed all over you, write down what your critics are saying and ask God to show you whether their charges have foundation.

- Did you do what He wanted you to do?
- Were you where He wanted you to be?

- Are you still doing what He wants you to do?
- Are you still where He wants you to be?

Look for evidence. A sharp pencil, a yellow legal pad, and probing questions have been some of the greatest tools in my life when I was blind-sided by biting criticism. Lost in the briars where words cut, it helps you retrace your steps as you look for trail markers back up the path that explain how you got to a place where you are criticized. Was that turn you made back up the trail a mistake? If it was, now is the time to know it, not later. Was it the right decision, given what you knew at the time? Is there evidence that it was the decision God wanted you to make? If it was, then now is the time you desperately need to know it.

With 20/20 hindsight, learn to "jot it down." After being lost, it's like finding the way. If what you jot down points to "this was the Lord," then God's word to your critics is: "Leave him alone . . . . It was intended that he serve Me this way."

THE REAL OBJECTIVE

If you are where you are supposed to be, doing what you are sup-posed to do—then what is done to you is really done to Another. Those barbs. Those verbal slaps. The digs. You don't take them alone. You take them with Him.

What was said at that dinner nearly two thousand years ago bumped into Someone besides Mary: "'Leave her alone,' said Jesus. 'Why are you bothering her? She has done a beautiful thing to me. The poor you will always have with you, and you can help them any time you want. But you will not always have me'" (Mark 14:6–7).

Like lightning that crackled the air, Jesus spoke. Why? Because He knew those outcries gunned at Mary shot like lasers targeted for Him. Those caustic words were meant to demean His lordship. They were intended to stop the worship that was rightly His. The criticism made Him look less than what He really was—God. The eleven who were sucked into the moment acted out of ignorance. Judas, who had never received the Lord, acted with evident intent. Either way, when Mary was criti-cized in her worship of the Lord, the words were an affront to Him.

Again, the principle: If you are where you are supposed to be, doing what you are supposed to do, then what is done to you is really done to Another. You don't take the punches alone; you take them with Him.

Do you remember what the Savior said to Paul (whose Jewish name was Saul) on the road to Damascus? "Saul, Saul, why do you persecute me?" (Acts 9:4). Paul's criticism of believers (which by this time had degenerated into barbarism) hurt Someone in addition to those Christians. It hurt the Lord. Was Jesus bodily present as with Mary at Simon's house? No. He was seated at the right hand of the Father in heaven. But the Lord *was* there! Paul's victims were members of His spiritual body. What was done to them was done to Him. He felt it! To tear away at one of our Lord's own—including you—is to claw away at Him.

Now that's a place to toss your anchor during a word typhoon. A servant does not serve alone. What happens to him or her happens to Another as well.

> He who receives you receives me, and he who receives me receives the one who sent me.
>
> —MATTHEW 10:40

> He who listens to you listens to me; he who rejects you rejects me; but he who rejects me rejects him who sent me.
>
> —LUKE 10:16

> I tell you the truth, whoever accepts anyone I send accepts me; and whoever accepts me accepts the one who sent me.
>
> —JOHN 13:20

When you are where you are supposed to be, doing what you are supposed to do, if you are received, *He* is received. If you are rejected—especially as a Judas rejects—*He* is rejected.

Our family lived in a neighborhood that we really enjoyed—with the exception of one neighbor. We tried to build bridges to this middle-aged lady, but she lit each one on fire. Finally, my wife and I thought we had at least a pedestrian walkway in place that opened the opportunity to talk to her about the Lord. I had repeatedly cleared snow from her sidewalks. Debbie had helped her with sewing projects, like getting ready for her son's wedding. But when we tried to share Christ with her and why her religious beliefs would not get her into heaven, that did it. The footbridge went up in a roar of flames.

From that day forward, like a chainsaw chewing up timber, she ripped our children apart before their playmates, once cussing them out over the fence while they were at play. It left my eleven-year-old in tears. No one had ever talked like that about her or her mother and father, not to mention the language used.

We had long talks with the children. We prayed for the lady. We explained that the lady was not acting with the mind of a fifty-year-old person. That helped, but not much. Only when we explained that our neighbor didn't like them because she didn't like us, did they understand. What the lady was doing to Carrie Anne, Brian, and Amy was really directed at us. "Because she refuses to accept Mama and Daddy, she refuses to accept you. To her, you are like us." That made sense. And so does this:

> Blessed are you when people insult you, persecute you and falsely say all kinds of evil against you because of me. Rejoice and be glad, because great is your reward in heaven, for in the same way they persecuted the prophets who were before you.
>
> —MATTHEW 5:11–12

That's comfort when taking Another's rap. You hate to think that verbal persecution slung your way comes from those you serve, especially if they claim to be followers of the Lord. But if they don't know the Lord, or know the Lord but are out of fellowship, it can happen. Not that your critics are aware of what they are really doing. From their perspective, they just don't like what you are doing. But if you are where you are supposed to be, doing what you are supposed to do—then what is done to you is really done to Another. Those barbs, verbal slaps, and digs; you don't take them alone. You take them with Him.

It's going to call for faith of the most radical sort. When you serve one who is into wholesale rejection, nothing less will do. You don't hear Christ's lightning-quick response as Mary did, knowing that what has been said distressed Him, too. You don't see the change in His expression. You don't detect the sober tone in His voice. There's no vindication for others to witness, much less for you to say, "I told you so." It's going to call for faith of the most radical sort, if you are where you are supposed to be, doing what you are supposed to do—to believe that what is done to you is really done to Another, and because it is, He will take care of it in His way and time.

Radical, radical faith is what it takes.

But it is that kind of faith that honors the Lord the most. It's that kind of faith that moves the Lord to reward the most. "And without faith it is impossible to please God, because anyone who comes to him must believe that he exists and that he rewards those who earnestly seek him" (Heb. 11:6).

James Lee Burke, the acclaimed novelist, wrote a book in the mid-1970s called *The Lost Get-Back Boogie*. The novel was rejected 111 times by New York publishers alone. In American publishing, it is still considered one of the most thoroughly rejected manuscripts. But with tenacity, Burke hung tough and eventually found one reluctant publishing house, Louisiana State University Press, to take a chance on his story. In 1985, James Lee Burke was nominated for a Pulitzer Prize for *The Lost Get-Back Boogie*.[5] Wouldn't it have been nice to have a few candid camera video clips of some New York publishers? What they considered unfit was close to perfect!

Don't kid yourself; you are not nearly perfect. But if you are where you are supposed to be, doing what you are supposed to do, you are heading in the right direction. It is then that what is done to you is really done to Another. You don't take the darts alone. You take them with Him. And He will reward, in His time and way . . . maybe even with a few video clips.

Therefore, "let us not become weary in doing good, for at the proper time we will reap a harvest if we do not give up" (Gal. 6:9).

NO SECOND-GUESSING

When left out at the curb, a lot of things go through your mind.

- "If I had done things differently, maybe it would have turned out better."

- "Maybe I should have done more."
- "Maybe I should have done more a whole lot sooner."

With a vengeance, the questions come. You relive it and relive it
. . . and relive it. You look at every angle. You take what happened,
and through your mental software, run it every which way. You wonder if another approach could have prevented what happened and
still allowed you to maintain integrity.

Mary was probably no different.

- "Maybe I should have asked the Lord in private first if it was all
  right."
- "I probably should have used the other perfume. It didn't cost
  as much. It would not have seemed so wasteful."
- "And the poor. I really do care about them. I could have sold
  this for no telling how much and fed needy families."
- "Besides, I could have. . . ."

"Leave her alone," said Jesus. "Why are you bothering her?
She has done a beautiful thing to me. The poor you will always have with you, and you can help them any time you
want. But you will not always have me. She did what she could."

                                                        —MARK 14:6–8A

Case closed.

Jesus' declaration suspended every question. That was the answer
that answered them all. No more wondering. No more sparring with
her thoughts. No more thinking, "Maybe the critics are right. What I
did was dumb." No more of that. Mary was a saint at peace.

Did you do what you could? Think back . . .

Did you use everything that you could think of at the time to resolve the problem?

Did you put full energy into it?

Were you like Mary in spirit—before the Lord as you said and did it?

Did you hold back in any area that you knew would make a
difference?

If you examine all that has taken place and you conclude that you could have done little more—then forget it. Wait until the judgment seat to hear the Lord's evaluation. His findings are what counts—not the complaints of those you serve.

> So then, men ought to regard us as servants of Christ and as those entrusted with the secret things of God. Now it is required that those who have been given a trust must prove faithful. I care very little if I am judged by you or by any human court; indeed, I do not even judge myself. My conscience is clear, but that does not make me innocent. It is the Lord who judges me. Therefore judge nothing before the appointed time; wait till the Lord comes. He will bring to light what is hidden in darkness and will expose the motives of men's hearts. At that time each will receive his praise from God.
>
> —1 CORINTHIANS 4:1–5

SAVED FACE

Veteran American League baseball umpire Bill Guthrie was working behind the plate one afternoon, and the catcher for the visiting team was repeatedly protesting his calls. Guthrie endured this for a number of innings and then called a halt. "Son," he said softly, "you've been a big help to me in calling balls and strikes today, and I appreciate it. But I think I've got the hang of it now, so I'm going to ask you to go to the clubhouse and show whoever's there how to take a shower."[6]

Wouldn't it be nice if God told your critic to hit the shower? Time to hang up your cleats. You're finished. No more of this.

He did for Mary. As the umpire of all words, actions, motives, and attitudes, He told that critical gang in a very nice way, "Game's over."

Perhaps the Lord is vindicating you before those you serve, and He has obviously come to your defense. What you did wasn't stupid. What you did was necessary. In fact, what you did looks quite good. Maybe He has vindicated you and, by doing so, said to your critic, "Game's over."

Or maybe not.

Even though things may be getting worse, the umpire of the universe may not have stepped in. For now, the game goes on. For you there has been no vindication.

If that's so, don't be disappointed. Often there are things He needs to teach His own, and outward vindication could conflict with that higher agenda. First things first.

But how can you keep on? How can you show your face to serve others when you've been nailed by some you serve? Undeserved humiliation can shut the best of us down, but it doesn't have to. We can still leave as Mary did—no shame, no reason to hide under the bed. If we came to worship Him through righteous motives, choices, and words, yet were severely criticized for it, we can leave with a face that is not ashamed.

How?

> Those who look to him are radiant;
> their faces are never covered with shame.
>
> —PSALM 34:5

Interested?

Join me in the next chapter.

Chapter 3

WHEN GOD DOESN'T DEFEND

The votes are in. The results are nine 'yes,' seven 'no,' and one 'over my dead body.'"

Where you work, possibly among peers, or in an actual vote taken by those you serve—have you been there and felt voted on like that? Your critics have been to the ballot box again and again to voice their estimation of you.

It's not all bad news. Likely, there are some "yes" votes. In some things your reviewers agree with you. And if they don't outwardly agree, at least they've chosen not to make an issue over all that you have said or done. Even though these are only implied "yes" votes, don't ignore them. Remember: just because someone turns negative does not mean that they've turned negative on everything. It's not all bad news.

But then there are some "no" votes. Fairly vocal. Maybe at first they surprised you, but hopefully you realize even in good ministry partnerships no two people are on the same page on every issue. Good ministry partnerships are made up of people who've learned to live with areas of inflexibility. Without compromising biblical core values, they've made peace with the way they are. Hopefully, you are learning that it's okay to be surprised by a "no." It's even okay to be disappointed or feel hurt by a "no."

But an "over my dead body" kind of "no"? That's the one that pushes the envelope. It's an "in-your-face" vote. It's an "I'm in your face, and I am going to stay in your face" vote. When a critic assumes that mind-set, life for the servant can become a living inferno.

That was Mary. She had worshiped the Lord with childlike simplicity, and it was over Judas's dead body that she would ever pull that stunt again.

> Six days before the Passover, Jesus arrived at Bethany, where Lazarus lived, whom Jesus had raised from the dead. Here a dinner was given in Jesus' honor. Martha served, while Lazarus was among those reclining at the table with him. Then Mary took about a pint of pure nard, an expensive perfume; she poured it on Jesus' feet and wiped his feet with her hair. And the house was filled with the fragrance of the perfume.
>
> But one of his disciples, Judas Iscariot, who was later to betray him, objected, "Why wasn't this perfume sold and the money given to the poor? It was worth a year's wages." He did not say this because he cared about the poor but because he was a thief; as keeper of the money bag, he used to help himself to what was put into it.
>
> –JOHN 12:1–6

"Over my dead body." Determined to shame Mary into oblivion, Judas publicly nailed her hide to the wall.

But he failed. No critic was able to put Mary to shame. What poured from her flask symbolized what overflowed from her heart—sheer worship. She loved the Lord. With all her heart, soul, mind, and strength, Mary loved the Lord. And the worshiped One wasn't about to let a betrayer and a few misguided followers grind this woman down into a pile of shame.

> "Leave her alone," said Jesus. "Why are you bothering her? She has done a beautiful thing to me. The poor you will always have with you, and you can help them any time you want. But you will not always have me. She did what she could. She poured perfume on my body beforehand to prepare for my burial. I tell you the truth, wherever the gospel is preached

throughout the world, what she has done will also be told, in memory of her."

—MARK 14:6-9

Criticism dismissed.

Case closed.

What was said was absolutely wrong. What was done was perfectly right. It was exoneration from no less than God Himself!

Mary came.

Mary was criticized.

Mary was vindicated.

Mary survived.

SURVIVE?

You, too, came and were criticized. Certainly it was not for doing what Mary did—the Lord is no longer bodily present to be anointed. But He's present to be worshiped, and hopefully what you did was in that spirit. What you did, you did for Him. What was done, was done the best you could.

And the response? Verbal stabs. Maybe, as with the eleven, your critics spoke in ignorance. But perhaps a cut came from one who has assumed the conscious "over my dead body" mind-set.

You came.

You were criticized.

You have yet to be vindicated.

And though vindication may not be what you seek, you still wonder if you will survive. Others who've heard about problems whisper, and you sense that a cloud hangs over you. The cracks in the ministry are because of you. The tension among those you serve is because of you. And there has been no outward evidence to indicate otherwise. You have not been vindicated. You have not been cleared. Can you really keep going on?

Mary could. One advantage that you and I do not have is that God was there for all to see. He issued His verdict for all to hear. On that day almost two thousand years ago, Mary did what she had to do, was condemned, and within seconds was acquitted.

She survived.

If you have been criticized without grounds, the vindication will come. Maybe soon. Maybe not so soon. Certainly in eternity. But what about the days, weeks, months, years, and even a lifetime between now and then? It's a jungle out there, and if you are not careful, you will get eaten alive—no peace, no enjoyment of life, no inner drive to press on—eaten alive with only a carcass for others to find.

How do you survive when heaven is quiet?

HARD QUESTIONS, AGAIN

- In 1902, the poetry editor of *Atlantic Monthly* returned a stack of poems with this note, "Our magazine has no room for your vigorous verse." The poet was Robert Frost.[1]
- In 1905, the University of Berne turned down a doctoral dissertation as "irrelevant and fanciful." The writer of that paper was Albert Einstein.[2]
- In 1894 an English teacher noted on a teenager's report card, "A conspicuous lack of success." The student was Winston Churchill.[3]

Rejected and vindicated for all to see. It's nice, isn't it, when others see in no uncertain terms that you are not a loser? But for now, that's not your story. So, how will you make it?

It certainly won't be by mentally rehashing the criticism. For sure, we need to talk it out, especially to the Lord. We are told: "Do not be anxious about anything, but in everything, by prayer and petition, with thanksgiving, present your requests to God" (Phil. 4:6). We need to tell Him.

But no rehash. That's declaring war on yourself. Your mind will blaze into a Hiroshima. To find peace for the long haul, we must grapple with issues more consequential than what is rehashed on the pillow. Issues like . . .

- Where was God in the midst of it all? When the charges flew, when the misquotes were made, when the insults were slung, where was He?

- What role did He play behind the scenes while we took the heat? With the hurt, the shock, the wave after wave of criticism crashing in, what was His part in all of it?
- Have we accepted His part in what has taken place? Even though left mangled. Even still living with the consequences. Even when others still may have no part with us. Given all of that, have we accepted what He did or did not do in the midst of it all?

We must dig our way past secondary causes, beyond the dirt, to bedrock where it's solid. We must find out where God is in all that has gone on. Then we must decide if we can live with what we find. How we embrace Him and His involvement in all that has gone on will determine whether we survive.

AN UNSEEN PRESENCE

In the sixth grade I helped other students cross the road during the thirty minutes before and the thirty minutes after school. I was a "patrol boy," with a badge, helmet, flagpole, and official raincoat. I stopped traffic. I stopped pedestrians.

Prominent, commanding, compelling, powerful—that may be overstating matters—but I had never felt so important.

Several peers, who did not get a badge, helmet, flagpole, and official raincoat due to grades, attitude, and a despicable lifestyle (as despicable as a sixth-grader's could be back then), changed that.

- "Look at Allen—a cop."
- "Where're your handcuffs?"
- "When you gonna come get us?"
- "Barney, did Andy give you your bullet today?"
- "Hey, look, we're crossin' the street when we ain't supposed to. Blow your whistle and arrest us."

Life was tough on the beat; I mean really tough. For days, the taunting went on. I couldn't tell my teacher; no self-respecting sixth-grade boy would ask a teacher to come to his rescue. But it was bad enough that I told my daddy. I was so rattled, I was ready to apply for early retirement.

You know what my father did to encourage me to hang in there? He parked his car about a half-block away each morning for several weeks. He never got out. He never said anything to anyone else. Nobody else even knew he was there. But I did, and did that ever make my day.

The more painful the hurt, the more likely the question: "Where is God?" This ministry match was made in heaven . . . you thought. Yet the cutting words, the displeasure expressed toward you, the emotional blood dripping from your soul is anything but from above. "Where is God?"

Intellectually, you know that He is right there, unseen and quiet. He's not making a discernible move, but He is there as much as you are. As Jesus was there, seeing and hearing all that went on when Mary was verbally kicked, so He is with you. He hears your critic's words. He sees your critic's expressions and gestures. He hears and sees it all.

> Where can I go from your Spirit?
> Where can I flee from your presence?
>
> If I go up to the heavens, you are there;
> if I make my bed in the depths, you are there.
>
> If I rise on the wings of the dawn,
> if I settle on the far side of the sea,
>
> even there your hand will guide me,
> your right hand will hold me fast.
>
> If I say, "Surely the darkness will hide me
> and the light become night around me,"
>
> even the darkness will not be dark to you;
> the night will shine like the day,
> for darkness is as light to you.
>
> —PSALM 139:7–12

Remember that first decisive shove your critic gave you, a shove right into the furnace? Totally unexpected, was it not? The Lord's omniscience kept Him "informed." He was aware of the ridicule. The insults were no surprise. A. W. Tozer wrote:

> God knows instantly and effortlessly all matter and all matters, all mind and every mind, all spirit and all spirits, all being and every being, all creaturehood and all creatures, every plurality and all pluralities, all law and every law, all relations, all causes, all thoughts, all mysteries, all enigmas, all feeling, all desires, every unuttered secret, all thrones and dominions, all personalities, all things visible and invisible in heaven and in earth, motion, space, time, life, death, good, evil, heaven, and hell.[4]

But God practices more than omniscience. In His omnipresence He has chosen to be near. Right there. He wants to see it all, though in His omniscience He *has* seen it all. He hears it *for the second time.* The novelty or intrigue of a situation does not appeal to a God who will never see or hear anything new; His being there is because He wants to be there, charge by charge. He wants to be there with you.

And surely I am with you always, to the very end of the age.
—MATTHEW 28:20B

I will not leave you as orphans; I will come to you.
—JOHN 14:18

God has said, "Never will I leave you; never will I forsake you."
—HEBREWS 13:5B

For the servant on the grill, that is comfort. Your Lord was not off somewhere else, absorbed with greater concerns than what you faced. He did not rely on angelic couriers to keep Him updated. No heavenly cell phones. You received His full attention, His full presence. Because God is spirit, there is no splitting Him up—a part here, a part over there—so that all can have a piece of His presence. He is indivisible. And because of that, wherever He is, His whole being is, His power, knowledge, wisdom, sovereignty, holiness, and love. All that God is, God is where He is, engaging Himself in perfect harmony as He uses His attributes. It's the uniqueness of omnipresence. That's your God. Totally undistracted, immersed in what is going on with you, as if you are the only one.

So settle it in your heart. The cutting words. The obvious displeasure. The emotional blood dripping from your soul. You did not go through what you went through (and maybe are still going through) alone. Your Lord was there. He wanted to be. "Even though I walk through the valley of the shadow of death, I will fear no evil, for you are with me; your rod and your staff, they comfort me" (Ps. 23:4).

Through your toughest time in ministry, which may be now—that's support. At this very moment, the Lord Himself is with you. He would not have it any other way.

BEHIND THE SCENES

As I stood solo at my patrol post, my father was right there with "all eyes" watching from his car. I was one grateful sixth-grade dude. His presence provided a moral support that I desperately needed. Just knowing he was there helped me with the taunts while out on the beat.

I still was on my own. Daddy never pulled any strings, never ran interference, never called the school to file a formal complaint. His presence was strictly for my own personal encouragement.

For us, too, God's presence is for our own personal encouragement . . . and infinitely more. He's there to make a difference.

He knows. He knows all that will happen in light of the criticism—the consequences for you, your family, and your ministry. He knows all the past, understanding completely how and why things came to this crisis. He knows the mistakes you made and what you did that was correct. He knows how others reacted and why. He heard when comments were made, the concerted effort to put the full-court press on you.

As He knows all the past, He certainly knows the way things are now. He knows how you feel, how you hurt. He knows what is going on in its totality at this moment.

He knows what could have been under other circumstances. He knows that a jog in the chain of events back up the road would have led to a completely different set of circumstances.

He knows what could be, all the possible outcomes given what is now happening. He knows the least painful and most painful options and what will actually result. He is not there with you to gather information; rather, it is because He *has* the information—all of it—that He is there.

Has someone you serve dragged out bones from your past? God already knew about those things, and He still wanted you as His servant. Has your critic zeroed in on some weakness in your makeup, exposing it for all to see? Others may be shocked, but not the Lord. Knowing all about it, He saved you. Tozer wrote:

> How unutterably sweet is the knowledge that our heavenly Father knows us completely. No talebearer can inform on us, no enemy can make an accusation stick; no forgotten skeleton can come tumbling out of some hidden closet to abash us and expose our past; no unsuspected weakness in our characters can come to light to turn God away from us, since he knew us utterly before we knew him and called us to himself in the full knowledge of everything that was against us.[5]

All things that are, were, will be, could have been, and could be, God knows, and He knows them equally well. Never stunned. Never surprised. No need to learn. No need to gather facts. He is not there to sit in the car monitoring your every move. Anything but.

> O LORD, you have searched me
> and you know me.
>
> You know when I sit and when I rise;
> you perceive my thoughts from afar.
>
> You discern my going out and my lying down;
> you are familiar with all my ways.

Before a word is on my tongue
you know it completely, O LORD.

You hem me in—behind and before;
you have laid your hand upon me.

Such knowledge is too wonderful for me,
too lofty for me to attain.

—PSALM 139:1-6

He knows how to use what He knows. He knows how to handle the "what will be," "what could have been," and "what could be" facts skillfully. He understands the proper relationship between each bit of information, no matter how infinitesimal.

It's not enough to know what to do. One must know how to do it. God does. He always does. Because He has goals for each of His children—goals commensurate with His nature—He will use the noblest possible means, given the facts, to achieve them. This is called wisdom. J. I. Packer writes: "Wisdom is the power to see, and the inclination to choose the best and highest goal, together with the surest means of attaining it."[6]

He knows what goal is best. And knowing it, He uses what is best to reach it. That includes the criticism:

- What is true and untrue in it.
- Whether the facts are being used carefully and correctly.
- Your critic's temperament.
- The brashness with which the criticism is made.
- The willingness or unwillingness of all sides to listen.
- What is being said publicly and privately and to whom.
- Your response to your critic's temperament.
- Your response to others in light of your critic's temperament.

He uses it all to achieve the goals that He has set for you as a believer in Christ.

Would we use such things? No way! If you could have prevented what took place, you would have. There would be no critic, criticism, or consequences. But if you really possessed His wisdom not a thing would change His goals for you, or the way He chooses to reach those goals for you, or the way He chooses to use "what now has taken place" to reach those goals for you.

Not a thing would change.

> All this also comes from the LORD Almighty,
> wonderful in counsel and magnificent in wisdom.
>
> —ISAIAH 28:29

> My purpose is that they may be encouraged in heart and united in love, so that they may have the full riches of complete understanding, in order that they may know the mystery of God, namely, Christ, in whom are hidden all the treasures of wisdom and knowledge.
>
> —COLOSSIANS 2:2-3

He is able to use what He knows. He could have prevented it all. The blow-up. The harsh words. The silence. God's power is such that He is able to do whatever He wants. He has the strength to stop what is taking place from happening.

There are things we would probably like to do now, such as make life as if the hurt never happened, removing from our memory all of the painful charges. But what we would like to do, and what we *can* do, are very different matters.

Not with God. If He desires to do it, it is done, and done without any effort. Nothing can stop Him. No devil. No demon. No person— not even your critic. His power simply cannot be short-circuited. It's called omnipotence.

Why didn't He use all that power to stop what took place?

His wisdom. Given His goals for each of His children, wisdom dictated that His power be displayed as it was—irrespective of what it might look like. If He had wanted to stop what happened, He would have. It wasn't because He couldn't. Omnipotence knows nothing of "couldn't." It wasn't because He was caught off guard. Omniscience takes care of that. The Lord did not stop it because His wisdom would not let Him stop it. What has happened or is happening fits right into His strategy for accomplishing His purposes.

The good. The bad. The ugly. It looks like a jigsaw puzzle still in the box, with no picture on the top to let you know what it is all supposed to look like when put together. God sees the finished work. He sees how every piece is strategic to that final image. Ignore a piece and you mess up a picture. In His wisdom, He will not do that. The Lord did not stop what has happened in your life because His wisdom knows that it is necessary to the total picture.

> Is anything too hard for the LORD?
>
> —GENESIS 18:14A

> The LORD brings death and makes alive;
> he brings down to the grave and raises up.
>
> —1 SAMUEL 2:6

> I make known the end from the beginning,
>   from ancient times, what is still to come.
> I say: My purpose will stand,
>   and I will do all that I please.
>
> —ISAIAH 46:10

He uses it. Because God is all-knowing, all-wise, and all-powerful, He alone rules and He rules all. From the electron spinning around the nucleus of the atom to the galaxies spinning out in space—everything smaller, greater, in-between, visible or invisible, He rules. His omnipresence, omniscience, wisdom, and omnipotence make it so. That includes what you are going through right now. Your ministry. Your critic. Your very critical critic. The cutting words. The obvious displeasure. The emotional blood dripping from your soul. He rules when people know it. He rules when people do not know it. He rules when it doesn't look like He's ruling.

Nothing happens that is not filtered through the rule of God. We both know it as *sovereignty*. In its absolute sense, sovereignty can be attributed only to God.

Again, Tozer:

God's sovereignty is the attribute by which He rules His entire creation, and to be sovereign God must be all-knowing. . . . Were there even one datum of knowledge, however small, unknown to God, His rule would break down at that point. To be Lord over all the creation, He must possess all knowledge. And were God lacking one infinitesimal modicum of power, that lack would end His reign and undo His kingdom; that one stray atom of power would belong to someone else and God would be a limited ruler and hence not sovereign.[7]

So does that mean that, since God is sovereign, His fingerprints are all over your ministry pain? The ultimate cause is Him? If He controls all, are we at best marionettes dangling from heaven's strings? Is not any talk of human culpability simply a sham? If His rule is really all-pervasive, is He not the catalyst for the criticism in the first place? How can anyone be held accountable for acts—including wrong acts—if we never had a choice in the matter? If God is sovereign, is not the antecedent reason for your critic's treatment of you, Him?

No. God is so great, He has the capacity to accomplish what He wants to accomplish, ruling over all that takes place, without violating either our freedom to choose or His perfect nature. How? Ultimately, only God knows. The secret things belong to Him (see Deut. 29:29).

If your ministry is in trouble, it's not because of God. It is because of you, your critic, other factors, or some intricate combination of influences. We all have choices. Your critic chooses what to say and do and how to say it and do it. You choose how you will receive that criticism and the response you will make. We all are granted wills that choose, which makes us responsible for what is chosen.

Since God is so great to maintain sovereignty in every detail, even as we exercise our freedoms to choose, He actively rules behind the scenes in all that we face. That includes you and your ministry. He will see to it that His purposes stand firm.

I encourage you, then, not to get lost in the secondary causes:

- "If he had not made it on the board, he would have never gotten his teeth into me."

- "If that family were not so influential in the church, no way would anyone listen to them."
- "If she were not on staff, and had not been raised in this church, the tension would evaporate."

If . . . if . . . if. . . . That's getting lost in collateral causes. True, perhaps if Mr. Know-It-All were not on the board, there would be peace. Perhaps you wouldn't get repeatedly sautéed if that family had left a long time ago. Possibly you would be in a less tense ministry with a different staff person. But none of those things have happened, and it isn't because God suffered a glitch in His sovereignty.

What did or did not happen down to the littlest detail, He ruled.

Remember what the Lord said to Pilate: "You would have no power over me if it were not given to you from above" (John 19:11a). And your critic (or critics)—including all that has contributed toward their behavior—would have no power over you if it were not given to him or her from above.

He or she may not know it.
Others may not know it.
But God does.
And now so do you.

> The LORD does whatever pleases him,
> in the heavens and on the earth,
> in the seas and all their depths.
>   —PSALM 135:6

> I make known the end from the beginning,
> from ancient times, what is still to come.

> I say: My purpose will stand,
> and I will do all that I please.
>   —ISAIAH 46:10

> All the peoples of the earth
> are regarded as nothing.

He does as he pleases
with the powers of heaven
and the peoples of the earth.

No one can hold back his hand
or say to him: "What have you done?"

—DANIEL 4:35

In him we were also chosen, having been predestined according to the plan of him who works out everything in confor-
mity with the purpose of his will.

—EPHESIANS 1:11

He uses what He knows perfectly. His knowledge, wisdom, power, and
sovereignty are never employed except in ways that are right.

But we may say, "What has happened is wrong. What was done to
me never should have taken place."

Wrong very possibly was done to you. What has been said and
done, whether intentional or unintentional, was either right or it was
wrong. In either case, God has chosen to use it and to use it for your
good (see Rom. 8:28). You are His house that He's framing. Unlike
the contractors we know, He will use lumber laced with termites.
God will use sin, without contaminating and implicating Himself. His
construction methods are simply beyond us. "Oh, the depth of the
riches of the wisdom and knowledge of God! How unsearchable his
judgments, and his paths beyond tracing out!" (Rom. 11:33).

- No mistakes.
- No mix-ups.
- No ulterior motives.
- No error in judgment.
- No sovereignty gone sour.
- No misuse of power.
- No lack of use when it should have been used.
- No wisdom that is defective.
- No knowledge that is imperfect.

Your critic acted as he or she did because, in His holy choices, God ruled as He did. He did not stop the person. He did not detach their tongues when they started speaking. He did not deafen you so that you would not hear, nor did he stop the ears of others who heard. He could have intervened. But to do so was not symmetrical with His holiness. What He chose to do or not to do was perfectly right. It wasn't a bad move. It wasn't neglect on His part. By decreeing both the end (holy goals for you) and the means (the use of fallen man's free choices in a fallen world), God has chosen exactly what you need.

> Your ways, O God, are holy.
> What god is so great as our God?
>
> —PSALM 77:13

And they were calling to one another:

> "Holy, holy, holy is the LORD Almighty;
> the whole earth is full of his glory."
>
> —ISAIAH 6:3

> For this is what the high and lofty One says—
> he who lives forever, whose name is holy:
>
> "I live in a high and holy place,
> but also with him who is contrite and lowly in spirit,
>
> to revive the spirit of the lowly
> and to revive the heart of the contrite."
>
> —ISAIAH 57:15

So what was God's role behind the scenes in all that has gone on? For sure, anything but a "view from the car." God makes a difference. He knows what is taking place and dictated a set of decisions that kept some things from happening while allowing others. He was the maestro, conducting it all. His power could have altered what has transpired, but He displays His power only in the way His wisdom deems best.

But was it best? Given the pain and damage done by a hypercritical tongue with the reciprocal fallout, was it really best?

Not if "best" is defined by what we feel. Not if "best" is defined by what we see. But if "best" is defined in terms of who God is, it has to be. He is the very definition of "best."

> Who will not fear you, O Lord,
> and bring glory to your name?
>
> For you alone are holy.
>
> All nations will come
> and worship before you,
>
> for your righteous acts have been revealed.
> —REVELATION 15:4

SELECTIVE RECEIVING

So where does that leave you? You've been severely criticized, without grounds. It hurts—you and maybe even others who look up to you. What was done came with a price tag, and you are paying on it now. In the light of God's working behind the scenes, where does it all leave you with your ministry?

If you see no further than your critic and his or her criticism, then you only compound the hurt.

- "I can't believe he would say that."
- "What a jerk—a real spiritual jerk."
- "There is no way she has any depth."

It goes on day after day. Then into weeks and months. And before you know it, years pass—life with it—and you still knead the pain.

- "Lies. That's all they were. Outright lies."
- "He was nothing but a clown. A farce."
- "What a failure. At best the IQ of a squid."

Like a mallet, you pound away. You beat it hard, sometimes harder than at other times, but always hard. At night. First thing in the morning. Anytime a conversation shows the slightest drift in that direction, you grab hold and set its course: "Do you know what he did to me . . . ?"

Pound.

Pound.

Pound.

But, do you know what you are pounding? Your own heart. With each blow, it gets harder and harder. Packed like steamrolled dirt. The air cannot get to it. The seeds of new truth won't germinate in it. What good growth remains won't be there much longer. The roots can't spread. The moisture of the Spirit does not reach it. The tender shoots of truth get clobbered, one by one.

That's the danger for a servant who ignores God's role behind the scenes.

But the one who does take into account God's role becomes a Mary—one who worships the Lord. No matter what it looked like to others, she was bringing out that flask. The oil would be poured. Her Lord was going to be anointed. So she worshiped. And though criticized, she left with face aglow.

Maybe you weren't worshiping in this way prior to the criticism. Maybe you were. It doesn't matter now. Pull your flask out. Anoint. In all that has taken place, your Lord has been, is, and will be nothing but Himself.

- Omnipresent
- Omniscient
- Wise
- Omnipotent
- Sovereign
- Holy

Loving, merciful, full of grace, immutable, truthful, good, faithful, kind, independent of all yet intimately acquainted with all, eternal, infinite, incomprehensible, preeminent, transcendent, majestic, patient, just, righteous . . . the one and only God. Though disgracefully criticized, you know the real bottom line:

"See, it is I who created the blacksmith
who fans the coals into flame
and forges a weapon fit for its work.

And it is I who have created the destroyer to work havoc;
no weapon forged against you will prevail,
and you will refute every tongue that accuses you.

This is the heritage of the servants of the LORD,
and this is their vindication from me,"
                                        declares the LORD.
                                        —ISAIAH 54:16–17

Worship.

Those who look to him are radiant;
their faces are never covered with shame.
                                        —PSALM 34:5

Chapter 4

WHEN YOUR CRITIC SPEAKS THE TRUTH

Sir, this message is for you. It's from the admiral."

"Sailor, then don't just stand there, read it."

"Of all the stupid, idiotic, asinine moves, yours takes the cake."

"Sailor, move it! Get that decoded at once!"

And we do. Whenever we hear what we don't want to hear, we decode the message at once.

We understand where the problem is—and it's not us.

But what if that's not reality? What if the way we understand the problem is not the way the problem really is? If there's life after another's words whip you to a bloody pulp, then nothing must deter us from seeing things as they really are—not even our pain. Reality must reign.

With electricity dancing across her voice, she said, "Pastor. There's been an accident."

"I'll be right there." And I was. It was bad—a crushed hip and leg—but it could have been a whole lot worse. The patient, sedated, was at rest. The wife, in a fuss, was not.

"Pastor, I will not let that doctor lay a hand on him. We're out of here. He won't let Tom take our vitamins while recovering from surgery. We've taken them every day for years, and Tom needs them more now than ever." And with that she began to make plans to have her husband transferred, calling around to find a physician who would merge her brew of megavitamins with standard post-surgical medications.

What if the doctor's concerns were well founded? What if a danger was posed by the interaction of huge doses of vitamins with other drugs? What if she was ignoring reality?

That did not matter to this sincere but misguided woman. The most important thing was to hear what she wanted to hear. Her husband hurt. Pain made truth irrelevant.

Moi?

- "You don't lead—you shove."
- "You say the same things over and over again."
- "The way you handled the situation made things much worse."
- "You've got a temper—and it's white-hot."
- "That was reckless. How could you do something like that?"
- "You scold people."
- "You said you would take care of it, but you didn't."
- "You don't identify with people."
- "You don't love people."
- "It would be nice if you would follow through."
- "When you speak, it's obvious you are not prepared."
- "You are a dictator."

Ouch. It's no fun hearing words like that, especially when they are smeared all over your name. It's report card time, and you didn't exactly make the honor roll.

But . . . I don't shove. . . . I do not say the same things over and over again. . . . It wasn't my response that made things worse. . . . I DON'T HAVE A TEMPER! . . . My actions were not reckless. . . . I don't scold; I advise. . . . I did take care of it. . . . I both identify with and love those I serve. . . . Follow through? Of course I follow through. . . . I study. I am prepared. . . . A Hitler? I'm no dictator!

Whom do you believe? After all, your critics have unleashed a wall cloud of pain. Like a tornado, they blew into your comfort zone, shredded your peace, tossed aside your discernment, and discounted your abilities. They took unauthorized inventory and found nothing of worth.

How could they storm your life and trash what's dear to you and blow it away?

So do you believe the hundred-mile-an-hour word twister, or the supporter who defends you at all cost? The answer is instinctive, but sometimes wrong. Just because we want to "decode" a message that makes us terribly uncomfortable does not mean that message is not true as stated. Pain ignores facts. It will attempt to adjust the truth. Pain tunes our ear to what it wants to hear.

Bottom line: "I'm out of this hospital. Me and my vitamins are going where we are wanted"—an attitude that will put you even deeper into an emotional grave.

To survive word battles, we must value what God values. When it comes to biblical axioms, none are more basic than the ones that deal with truth.

Surely you desire truth in the inner parts.

—PSALM 51:6A

The LORD is near to all who call on him, to all who call on him in truth.

—PSALM 145:18

Buy the truth and do not sell it.

—PROVERBS 23:23A

Stand firm then, with the belt of truth buckled around your waist.

—EPHESIANS 6:14A

There is nothing more basic than truth.

SPATIAL DISORIENTATION

The headline read, "'Pilot Failure Blamed in JFK Jr. Crash."[1] On July 16, 1999, John Kennedy Jr.'s plane plunged into the Atlantic Ocean off Martha's Vineyard, Massachusetts. He, his wife, and her sister perished. It happened on a flight from New Jersey as Kennedy prepared the Piper Saratoga II for the initial descent to land.

> In a brief report, released on the NTSB web site, the board said the probable cause of the crash was "the Pilot's failure to maintain control of the airplane during a descent over water at night, which was a result of spatial disorientation. Factors in the accident were haze and the dark night."
>
> Kennedy basically succumbed to a problem that has killed many pilots. At night in haze, with no horizon, stars or ground lights to provide orientation, a pilot must rely carefully on instruments. The mind can play tricks that make a pilot believe he is flying level when he may well be in a tight turn or even upside down.[2]

Spatial disorientation. That's what can happen to us when we try to land emotionally after getting hazed by another's words. It's night, and we lose our spiritual horizon. The mind plays tricks on us. We think we are flying level. We think our response to those bitter words is appropriate. But unless we rely carefully on the instruments of God's Word, we "may well be in a tight turn or even upside down."

Let's be honest. Our instinctive bent is to continue to believe what we already believe. We are our own greatest fans. We are also our own greatest stooges. Anything we try to sell to ourselves, we will buy.

If the criticism we face has at least some truth to it, now is the time to find out. We want to stop the hurt. We want to stop the bleeding. We want to press on in ministry. If what's being said has no truth to it, now is the time to settle that, too. It's foolish to hurt for the wrong reasons.

Flight instruments from God's Word help us see things as they really are. With them are readings that distinguish valid from invalid criticism. If truth is what your critics spoke, you will know it from the instruments. If something less than truth is what your critics spoke, you will know that from the instruments, too. The servant of God can honestly appraise what is said. In the midst of the hurt, God's Word keeps us on course.

The following are some flight instruments to watch when criticized so as to stay level and out of the tank.

TRUTHFULNESS: *Is Your Critic Trustworthy?*

I heard a pastor from Mobile, Alabama, share that he found a purse on the steps of his church building after services on a Wednesday evening. Inside the purse was a twenty-dollar bill with a phone number clipped to it. The pastor immediately returned to his office and called the number. He was told to go across the street to a parked van. When he did, he discovered a camera crew from a television network taping the whole episode for a special on *honesty*. The pastor found out that the producers had planted twelve purses in Mobile, including the one at his church door.

He asked how Mobile had done and received a fairly positive report. Then the network crew mentioned that in another community, where four purses were planted, only one was returned. However, that one "honest" person insisted on seeing the video: "You can't show that," he begged. "The woman whose hand I am holding . . . is not my wife." Yes, he returned the purse, but was he trustworthy?

Is your critic trustworthy? As a servant, you want to think the best of people. In fact, love does all it can to think the very best of people (see 1 Cor. 13:7). But when it comes to harsh charges and trying to discern truth in those charges, we need to ask with care the *trustworthy* question to know how much weight to give to what is being said.

True criticism comes from a truthful critic, whether the critic is colleague, fellow worshiper, or spouse.

"Blaine, is that not just pointing out the obvious?"

Maybe. But it is the foremost way to sort through all that you are hearing, and it is also scriptural. "A truthful witness gives honest testimony, but a false witness tells lies" (Prov. 12:17). That proverb reminds us that there's a link between what is said and who said it. It tells us that the character of the critic configures the character of the criticism. Truth comes from a person who is truthful. Something less than truth comes from a person who is not. Not that everything communicated by the latter is wrong; it's just that his words compared to the righteous man's words are not of the same caliber.

The mouth of the righteous is a fountain of life.

—PROVERBS 10:11A

The tongue of the righteous is choice silver.

—PROVERBS 10:20A

The lips of the righteous nourish many.

—PROVERBS 10:21A

The mouth of the righteous brings forth wisdom.

—PROVERBS 10:31A

The lips of the righteous know what is fitting.

—PROVERBS 10:32A

Is everything the righteous says correct? Of course not. He is not infallible. But because he values truth in life, his speech trait will be truth in life. Words are an overflow. "The good man brings good things out of the good stored up in his heart, and the evil man brings evil things out of the evil stored up in his heart. For out of the over-flow of his heart his mouth speaks" (Luke 6:45).

So in weighing criticism, we must weigh the character of the critic. Is he a truthful and, therefore, trustworthy witness?

As applied to those you serve, if you can assume that the person making the charge is generally truthful, it's probable that what they have said about you is so, at least as they see it. Maybe it could have been said more tactfully, with a different emphasis and tone. But it's still probably accurate, and you need to look closely and take to heart what has been said about you.

If you are not ready to acknowledge that what has been said by those you serve is true, then you raise a cloud of doubt over their spiritual health. That's serious, and you had better think whether you've seen this cloud over them with other issues as well. Character flaws are not closet flaws. They sneak out.

What have you noticed about your critic's integrity? Does he keep his word? Have you noticed a willingness to say "I was wrong," or is it always, always, always other people who are wrong? Is what she does done well? If the subject of honesty came up among others, would this person's name materialize as a paradigm?

Does the one who has been critical of you respect authority? Are there frequent problems with those in leadership? Is there a submissive spirit? If your critic is married, do you see a submissive spirit within that marriage, especially the wife toward the headship of her husband? Would the one who has turned seemingly harsh toward you model a genuine respect for government? For church elders and deacons? For church staff?

When it comes to facts, does your critic stick to them without additions or subtractions? Does he manipulate facts to bolster an argument? Do others count the critic's word as fact?

Does this person seem to be above reproach in the area of sexual morality? Is there any hint of unfaithfulness to his or her spouse? Do you have any reason to believe that this person might be into pornography? Would this person laugh at or tell off-color jokes? Would this person avoid even the appearance of impurity? From what you know, does this person rejoice over what is pure and grieve over what is not?

Questions like these help us discern the truth when we are having a hard time believing that what is said is the truth. Certainly we won't bat a thousand with all questions. Only the Lord knows what really is inside us. Nor are we looking to put on judicial robes. Those belong to God alone. But we are to be discerning. David said, "Let a righteous man strike me—it is a kindness; let him rebuke me—it is oil on my head. My head will not refuse it" (Ps. 141:5a–b). If, as far as you know, your critic would pass questions like these, then don't do the knee-jerk and automatically discount what is said.

A father polar bear and his son polar bear were taking in the last rays of an Arctic sunset. The kid asked, "Dad, am I one hundred percent polar bear?"

The father polar bear replied, "Of course, son—one hundred percent polar bear to the core."

About ten minutes later the son turned to his father again: "Dad, tell me the truth and nothing less. I can handle it. Am I one hundred percent polar bear? No brown bear, no black bear, no grizzly bear?"

The father replied, "Son, I'm one hundred percent polar bear, your mother is one hundred percent polar bear, so there is no way you can be anything else but one hundred percent polar bear, too."

A few minutes later the son turned to his father and said, "Dad, don't spare my feelings if it's not so. I gotta know—am I one hundred percent polar bear?"

The father, distressed by his son's doubts, asked, "Why do you keep wondering if you are one hundred percent polar bear?"

The son replied, "Because I'm freezing."

Friend, you may be freezing now from frigid words that left you numb. And even after deciding that a critic is generally truthful, you might still find it hard to believe that what they tell you is really so. But if you have no reason to doubt that your critic is, by the grace of God, one-hundred percent character to the core, you are smart to take seriously the criticism. The cleaner the bill of spiritual health, the more credible your critic's words.

EMPATHY: *Is Your Critic Concerned?*

"This is going to hurt me more than it is going to hurt you."

"If I did not care about you, I would not say it."

"This is tough, but I feel it is my place to point it out."

When any critic starts out like that, watch out! You are in for an emotional holdup. It's extortion. He wants you to think that his concern for you—even at the cost of great personal pain—obligates you to accept what he says.

Baloney. That is one of the oldest tricks in the book.

Yet *genuine* concern—empathy—on the part of the critic is an indicator that what is being said has validity. "A friend loves at all times, and a brother is born for adversity" (Prov. 17:17). "Wounds from a friend can be trusted, but an enemy multiplies kisses" (27:6). If the doctor removed an infected appendix, leaving you in pain for several weeks, would you consider him your enemy? Of course not. He did what was necessary for your overall wellbeing.

Ditto that with a friend, and count yourself blessed if your critic is a genuine friend. If they are truly concerned about you, it's your pain that is monitored, not theirs. They will stay with you through the process. Their feelings toward you will not be conditioned upon your feelings toward their criticism. That's genuine friendship.

The quality of a relationship prior to the criticism is important in analyzing the worth of what is said. The stronger the bond, the weightier the worth of the criticism. Not that criticism from casual contacts can be mechanically dismissed. Chance acquaintances can certainly make valid observations that we can use for our own betterment. But when you hurt—surgery without anesthesia—the remarks of friends should carry heavier weight. Most likely those comments cause wounds that, if received properly, will heal.

I was told in the early stages of ministry that I was leading by bullying others. I didn't like to hear that, so I didn't pay much attention. The critic had seen me in a Friday night conference leadership role—one of only a few times that he had seen me at all. It would take more than a one-night observation to persuade me.

I was told later that I was too quick with my tongue. I didn't like that, either. I was the model pastor. How could anyone accuse me of machine gun speech?

But deep down I knew the critic was right. She was my wife.

Listen to friends. Don't infer that their criticism means their distancing. Don't take it as a turn against you. And, for sure, don't automatically dismiss what is said. They may not be right, but they may not be all wrong either. "Better is open rebuke than hidden love" (Prov. 27:5).

COMPETENCE: *Is Your Critic Knowledgeable?*

Thomas Edison said, "If we all did the things we are capable of doing, we would literally astound ourselves."

Some critics don't even have to do that, and they still astound themselves. They already know everything about every subject. If that is where your critic is, both of you are to be pitied—the critic for having such a blinding arrogance and you for having to listen to it.

It is easy to get upset if the person dishing it out works from a small dish. When your critics don't know what they are talking about, their words are certainly suspect. It isn't so much a matter of not having the facts, as it is not knowing what to do with the facts if they did have them.

Do your best to determine if your critics know what they are talking about—not so much the specific remarks made pertaining to you, but the area of their concern.

Does your critic know something about leadership? Does the person hold a position of authority and responsibility at work? Is scripture affirmed through the leadership principles he or she is transferring from his or her job experience to your ministry?

Does your critic know something about speaking? Has he or she heard a lot of sermons or listened to outstanding Christian communicators on radio or television? Does the criticism come because you don't speak time after time like them, or has he or she picked up on some basic communication techniques that you would do well to learn from?

Whatever the area of the criticism, think about how much your critic knows and the source of what knowledge is there. This may not be easily assessed, but the question still needs to be answered as objectively as possible: Are those whose words seem so hard to you qualified to speak?

That does not mean that we shouldn't pay attention to someone who seems to know little. These persons may have much of value to say. To dismiss those with less formal training is sheer arrogance. Balaam had the opportunity to learn much from his donkey, with his refusal leaving some doubt as to who really was the stubborn old mule (see Num. 22:21–35).

However, criticism on a given subject normally assumes a knowledgeable critic on that given subject. If your critic has proven skills, then take the correction seriously. If the person does have an aptitude in the area where questions are raised, don't blow him or her off. To the best of your ability, come up with a fair portfolio assessing your critic's strengths.

After a husband criticized his son's homework grades and blamed his wife for not helping the child more, the wife said: "Well, do something about it. Help him while you can. Next year he will be in the third grade."

There is too much loose criticism floating around from people who think they know much more than they do. That may include the one who has found fault with you. The critique may sound impressive, even spiritual. But that doesn't earn acceptance at face value. Your critic should have a grasp of the issue and knowledge to be able to work with you beyond the early grades.

The Bible says, "Every prudent man acts out of knowledge, but a fool exposes his folly" (Prov. 13:16). That's worth remembering when you come under fire.

ACCURACY: *Is the Criticism Accurate?*

By now we have looked at your critic; hopefully with an uncritical spirit. We've reflected on his truthfulness, empathy, and competence for one reason: to find the best reading possible on what he says. Now we must go beyond the one who has found a weakness. Your critic has spoken—maybe a lot. It's time to survey the burden of his or her heart:

- What was said?
- Can it be documented?
- Is it true?

Yes? Then it's worth losing sleep over. If your critic is laser right, don't deny it. You hurt no one but yourself.

No? Then don't let it eat at you. Feeling bad when you don't need to feel bad is ridiculous. The Lord never did, and neither should His followers. If the criticism involves *measurable* behavior, you, more than anyone else, should know whether it is accurate.

- "You did not follow procedures."
- "You did not ask others on the team."
- "You told me you would do it."

What about it . . . ?

- You *did* follow procedures, and you have the documentation to prove it.
- You *did* consult with other team members.
- You *never told* your critic that you would do it.

Then relax. You may need to correct your critic gently on the facts, but don't let illegitimate criticism fester into feelings of anger, guilt, or worthlessness. Simply analyze what was said: Is it accurate?

If it is not accurate, though, don't be too quick to cry "Foul!" It's possible that you and the one God has called you to serve are not working from the same set of facts. When that is so, misunderstanding is inevitable.

Of course, both sides may be working from the same set of facts with one or both parties putting a different spin on them. That spells trouble. In an attempt to manage outcome, truth is manipulated. Remember: Others may put a twist on the facts; for the sake of truth you cannot.

And what is a telltale sign of fact-spinners? Absolute charges:

- "You *always* do it."
- "You *never* listen."
- "*Invariably* you do the same."
- "You are *forever* causing problems."
- "You are at it *continually*."

Those words shout that somebody is pressuring the facts. If your critic uses them, it's naïve not to have misgivings. Always? Never? Invariably? Forever? Continually? Nobody is that consistent. If you use such terms, stop it. That kind of thesaurus betrays a disposition that won't stomach truth.

Hard evidence turns up fairly easily when behavior is *measurable.* However, when it comes to the criticism of attitudes, facts are harder to come by. Suppose you are criticized for a "don't care" attitude, and it isn't the first time you have heard that complaint. At a previous ministry the same charge was leveled but in different words: "You don't follow through with assignments. Others are having to go behind you to make sure it's done right." After moving to another place, you hear it again: "It's like you don't care how things are done." When independent sources say the same thing, pay attention.

But if you hear it from one source and nowhere else, question marks may be in order. Be open enough to allow that this may be your critic's genuine and legitimate concern. There really may be a problem. But it may be a problem that's less important than your critic thinks. In the sight of God, it may not be a problem at all.

Take time to ask—Is the criticism accurate? Then take time to answer it with brutal honesty, even if it hurts. If evidence indicates you are in the wrong, admit it. That's the quickest way to climb out of an emotional grave.

RESTRAINT: *Was the Delivery of the Criticism Restrained?*

A husband remarked, "My wife is very touchy. The least little thing sets her off."

"You are fortunate," said the other man. "Mine is a self-starter."

And those who have expressed concerns that pertain to you—what was their emotional state? How were their allegations communicated? What was their temperature and the temperature of their words? Were they self-starters?

> Reckless words pierce like a sword,
> but the tongue of the wise brings healing.
> —PROVERBS 12:18

> The tongue of the wise commends knowledge,
> but the mouth of the fool gushes folly.
> —PROVERBS 15:2

> The heart of the righteous weighs its answers,
> but the mouth of the wicked gushes evil.
> —PROVERBS 15:28

> A man of knowledge uses words with restraint,
> and a man of understanding is even-tempered.
> —PROVERBS 17:27

Your critic's delivery is a good gauge to appraise what was delivered. Was he or she hot?

- "And another thing . . . !"

- "Don't give me any excuses."
- "You wait—I'm not finished yet."
- "This is the very last straw."
- "You ought to know better."
- "Look at the mess you've made!"

Reckless words. Angry words. A self-starter. They've gone from "warm" to "boil" in no time flat. It's no fun getting scalded like that.

Your critic is probably delivering one of the greatest sermons he or she will live to regret. It has been pointed out that anger is just one letter short of danger. Will Rogers said, "People who fly into a rage always make a bad landing."

Wise critics won't do that. They steer their words with restraint that reflects a tremendous sense of responsibility. They will not shout or intimidate you into raising a white flag. They will not dominate the conversation. A wise critic will want to hear your point of view.

They are cautious—they do not want to attack your self worth. They curb their remarks according to your reaction. In the midst of their criticism they will reinforce your positive points. You sense a commitment on their part to hang in there with you to achieve a good outcome.

- "How do you feel about it?"
- "May I make a few suggestions?"
- "Could you explain to me more about what took place?"
- "It will take time, but we will work it out."
- "I know this pains you; I would feel the same."
- "Do you have any thoughts as to where we might go from here?"
- "You know—I still think you are the greatest."

Value people who know how to criticize with compassion. Chances are they have been where you are—maybe with other people, possibly even with you. They know what it is like to be hung out to dry.

This is not to say that anger automatically invalidates criticism. The one who has it in for you may not know better. Perhaps emotions got the best of him or her. Or maybe you really blew it! As a general rule, the more severe the problem, the more emotional the critic.

Listen to Paul:

> When Peter came to Antioch, I opposed him to his face, because he was clearly in the wrong. Before certain men came from James, he used to eat with the Gentiles. But when they arrived, he began to draw back and separate himself from the Gentiles because he was afraid of those who belonged to the circumcision group. The other Jews joined him in his hypocrisy, so that by their hypocrisy even Barnabas was led astray.
>
> When I saw that they were not acting in line with the truth of the gospel, I said to Peter in front of them all, "You are a Jew, yet you live like a Gentile and not like a Jew. How is it, then, that you force Gentiles to follow Jewish customs?"
>
> —GALATIANS 2:11-14

Paul was fit to be tied and rightly so. By his actions Peter had implied that the gospel was not the good news of grace, but of grace *and* law. When a leader of Peter's stature compromised the gospel, Paul had every right to ignite. The issue was critical.

If you have blown it big-time, the heat you feel could very well be righteous indignation. But even then, let's hope it's tempered with compassion, the goal being to denounce the sin, not the sinner.

But you know as well as I do that most indignation is not righteous. Balance what has been said with the way it was said. That will help size up the legitimacy of criticism.

PAIN: *Does the Criticism Hurt?*

Abused healthy tissue hurts, but not as quickly as abused unhealthy tissue. We protect an infected finger, an inflamed toe, an arthritic knee at all cost. With diseased tissue, the slightest trauma sends us through the ceiling.

If there is no basis for what is said, words pound on healthy tissue—and, yes, it hurts. We must live with the consequences of the wrong done. We must adjust to the reality of the new situation. That can be tough. But the tissue itself, assuming a biblical response, will heal.

When there is infection under the skin, however, watch out. It's swollen. It's inflamed. Just the slightest critical touch and "Noooooooooo!" Unbearable agony. Excruciating. Sheer torture.

How much criticism can you take before you start to feel pain? Do you get madder every time you think about it? How often is "every time you think about it"? Inside, did you shriek? Are you still shrieking?

These are truth serum questions—they force us to raise the hardest issue of all: Could I really be in the wrong? Where there is a need for correction, truth will always hurt. Those first words of criticism bring something to light that we were not aware of and perhaps did not want to be aware of. Either way, it's a shock to our emotional system that should lead to a change—in the context of sin, a change called repentance.

Sometimes we balk. We go to any extreme to protect the lesion. Result? The infection spreads.

Don't simply live with the infection. Just remember: if what is said hurts, the pain may indicate tender tissue. Granted, some subject matter is meant to be sensitive. Eyes were not made to take a lot of poking. Some areas of life are not made for jabbing either. But tender tissue could indicate something else. If it does, lance the sore. Listen, take stock, and change.

OKTOC ROAD

I smelled it as I drove along on Oktoc, a sparsely populated two-lane road. Nighttime, and with windows down, it was a foul smell. It had to be a skunk out in the woods. The little critter must have gotten ticked off about something. A quarter mile down the road, I still smelled it. A half mile, three quarters, a full mile, and it was still in the air. Down my driveway and right into the garage, and the odor just about did me in. Then the cerebral lights came on: Without realizing it, I had hit a skunk. The stink was me, and I did not know it.

Friend, could it be possible the stink is in you, and you do not know it? What your critic said is really so, and the smell is bad. That's what this chapter is all about: to allow for that possibility. It's an attempt to make a reality search, to find out how things really are. If there's life after a word-walloping, you must embrace valid criticism.

To ignore it is to assume you don't need it. You've got your critic figured out. You know what she's really like; you know where he's coming from. Case closed. And you abscess with resentment that eventually breaks out into anger toward innocent people, including those you love the most.

Do a reality search. Know that spatial disorientation is always a possibility no matter how spiritual you are. Check the readings on your instruments:

- Truthfulness: Is your critic trustworthy?
- Empathy: Is your critic concerned?
- Competence: Is your critic knowledgeable?
- Factualness: Is the criticism accurate?
- Restraint: Was the delivery of the criticism restrained?
- Pain: Does the criticism hurt?

The preacher said, "Do not pay attention to every word people say, or you may hear your servant cursing you—for you know in your heart that many times you yourself have cursed others" (Eccl. 7:21–22). Indeed, wise counsel. Believe every critical word about you, and you will go bonkers. You cannot afford to let your mind become a freeway.

But the preacher in Ecclesiastes did not say, "Pay attention to *no* word." There are some critical words worth thinking about; things said that are worth taking the time to sort through. Among all that you hear, the trick is to know the difference and then to know what to do.

Friend, learn to eat the fish and spit out the bones.

Chapter 5

WHEN TO BLOW IT OFF

You will meet a beautiful young lady who will want to know everything about you," said the psychic to the frog who had telephoned her hotline.

"That's fabulous. Where will I meet her? In the park, along the seashore, on the trail to the woods?"

"No," countered the psychic. "Next semester in her biology class."

And that's no fun. Diced to pieces by another on a cold lab table, dissected until your emotional guts hang out. That's just no fun.

Someone has said, "Two things are hard on the heart—running uphill and running down people."

May I suggest a third? Running down yourself.

Unjust criticism—the untrue, excruciating, vicious, Biology 101 criticism—slashes deep. Though the critic may be gone, the gore is not.

- "Am I really that bad?"
- "Why did it happen that way? It must be because of me."
- "I just can't seem to do anything right."
- "I must not have what it takes."

In no time, the criticized has turned on himself, a cannibal's nightmare. And with an insatiable appetite, the impeached proceeds to consume what remaining shreds of emotional flesh are left.

- "Why continue?"
- "Who really wants or even needs me?"
- "What a failure, an ugly failure, I am."

Brutal words wheeled by brutal thoughts . . . and another victim is clubbed to a heartrending death. Of course, followers of the Lord should expect unfair treatment. It is part of the Christian career opportunity. Timothy was reminded by the Apostle Paul:

> You, however, know all about my teaching, my way of life, my purpose, faith, patience, love, endurance, persecutions, sufferings—what kinds of things happened to me in Antioch, Iconium and Lystra, the persecutions I endured. Yet the Lord rescued me from all of them. In fact, everyone who wants to live a godly life in Christ Jesus will be persecuted.
>
> —2 TIMOTHY 3:10-12

Jesus taught, in what is probably His most famous sermon:

> Blessed are those who are persecuted because of righteousness, for theirs is the kingdom of heaven. Blessed are you when people insult you, persecute you and falsely say all kinds of evil against you because of me.
>
> —MATTHEW 5:10-11

Ridicule, slander, sarcasm, contempt—it comes with the turf, along with the pain, doubts, and devastating self-appraisals. Someone speaks her mind, and the words fire like a demon from the abyss. The heat melts. We give way and droop. What is said is nothing short of an oven blast. Now we are scraps, junk, molten pain. We are ashes. Our critic told us so, and we believe the criticism.

There's got to be a better way. Since biased criticism will increase the more we grow in the likeness of our Lord and take seriously His call, there must be a better way to mentally handle what is vented.

THERAPY FOR THE BRUISED PSYCHE

There is—a biblical way. Paul was often the prey of stabbing tongues, and it wasn't all from unbelievers. One of the sickest New Testament churches labeled the great Apostle Paul an absolute failure.

- Paul, you don't know how to speak.
- Paul, you are not really an apostle.
- Paul, you are not very gifted.
- Paul, you don't know how to lead.
- Paul, with your handicap, you leave a bad impression.
- Paul, as we rank you with others, you don't measure up. You're just not effective.

Rumors like that had to hurt, especially from a people Paul had shepherded to the Lord and spent much time encouraging in their new faith.

The Corinthians took the apostle apart piece by piece. It was Biology 101, and he was the subject being verbally dissected. Nothing was sacred. Nothing. It is a wonder you and I ever heard of the man after what that church did to him. Laying him out on their cold lab table in one bloody mess, the Corinthians decreed: "You're a failure, Paul, and you need to know it . . . an absolute failure."

He didn't know it and had no intentions of knowing it. Read his response:

> So then, men ought to regard us as servants of Christ and as those entrusted with the secret things of God. Now it is required that those who have been given a trust must prove faithful. I care very little if I am judged by you or by any human court; indeed, I do not even judge myself. My conscience is clear, but that does not make me innocent. It is the Lord who judges me. Therefore judge nothing before the appointed time; wait till the Lord comes. He will bring to light what is hidden in darkness and will expose the motives of men's hearts. At that time each will receive his praise from God.
>
> —1 CORINTHIANS 4:1–5

Polite, courteous, but to the point: "I don't care." When evident that the detractors were not heaven's messengers, the apostle mentally blew it off. "I care very little if I am judged by you or by any human court." The man just kept walking, and he didn't walk all over himself.

The following will keep your shoes where they belong.

KNOW WHO YOU ARE

As Ralph drove down the freeway, the cell phone rang: "Ralph, this is your wife. I just heard on the news that some idiot is driving the wrong way down I-95. Be careful."

"Hazel, it's not just one car . . . there's hundreds of them."

Perspective often determines outcome. And when you are the recipient of in-your-face criticism, that is especially so. The way you and I view ourselves determines how well we handle harsh words.

We live and minister at a time when the Western evangelical church is making a historic paradigm shift. Less and less, Scripture is our sole authority. More and more, a culture that mirrors an antibiblical value system has the final say. In the name of relevance, demographic research determines our music and the shape of our message so that we can reinvent ourselves to appeal to the greatest number. Though perhaps done from positive motives, the results are staggering: The audience is not just the customer, it has been crowned sovereign king. "Do it this way. . . . We don't like it done that way. . . . Don't forget, we can vote with our pocketbook and our feet." Sovereign king.

To take the heat in the midst of such a radical shift and live to tell about it, we must understand and embrace heaven's perspective on servanthood. We must hear again the *true* sovereign King's stance on those who lead for Him. With it, we can endure for the long haul, no matter how "worldly" our Lord's bride becomes.

Paul knew that perspective. Though Paul's response to criticism in 1 Corinthians 4 is not the primary gallery of God's thoughts toward his own, there are some unforgettable portraits, like the two viewed in verse 1: "So then, men ought to regard us as servants of Christ and as those entrusted with the secret things of God."

Servants of Christ. "Yes," you say, "that's what I am."

Great. That's what I am, too . . . some of the time.

Only when I look closer at what a servant really is, I'm confronted with a troubling feeling that this snapshot is not always me. The photo is not of a person running one of heaven's regional offices as vice-president of operations. It's not an executive setting the vision and agenda for the kingdom from corporate headquarters. Based on Paul's choice of words from the original, a servant is a person clothed in sweat and the stench that comes along with it. This is a take-orders trench person doing what another tells him to do without raising an eyebrow. It was an expression used in Paul's day to depict those who rowed from the lowest tier in the belly of the ship, an odious, painful place to be.

And as an authentic servant of Jesus Christ, you row. Not as a favor, but because it's your place. Assignments are made, not choices given; chores are done, not careers chased. With love, for sure—love for the Master with all your heart, soul, mind, and strength—but a love that finds expression through the bent knee. You do what you are told even if no one else does it with you. You do it when others wouldn't dare. You do it unrecognized. You do it unappreciated. You just do it because you are His servant at His beck and call. If there are laurels for what was ordered, you know Who really deserves them. If there is something less . . . after thinking about it, you are not surprised; that's part of being a servant. Jesus said so: "So you also, when you have done everything you were told to do, should say, 'We are unworthy servants; we have only done our duty'" (Luke 17:10).

So what is really bothering you?

Are you reeling from the shock of unscrupulous criticism? That's understandable. But adjusting to the reality of "now," is there anything else that has bent you out of shape? Do the reverberations from what others think, say, and do torment you? Does the thought of facing people who've heard things that simply are not true horrify you? Are you afraid that the words that gored will cost you advancement, your job, not to mention friends and you just cannot shake it? To stagger from the shock is again understandable. But to stagger from more than shock may indicate that you cannot say with Paul, "I care very little," because you are an honest person, and you really care a whole lot.

Servants don't care a whole lot. What they do, they do because of the Master. It is the Master's responsibility to handle the fallout. The burden is His, not the servant's, to control the critic and grapple with the repercussions.

So what if you have encouraged, supported, and even wept with your critic, who has now taken a hunk out of your hide? You did not choose to serve your critic; God made that choice. Your choice was to be a servant. He assigned to you the task to serve someone He knew would bite the hand that fed it. As an unworthy servant, you only did your duty. You did what you were told to do.

Where I live they still ride on the back of the truck. Stopping at every house along the way, the two men do what few really want to do. Sometimes it's to pick up an end table, footstool, maybe a bench . . . stuff that looks pretty good to me. At other times it's to pick up what smells foul. But the two do what they are supposed to do, even if what's picked up is covered with maggots. As servants of Waste Management, these men just do not care a whole lot.

But me? When I walk through our neighborhood, I have been known to check out a rocking chair at the curb, a wheelbarrow, even a rake, just to see if it's something I could use. But garbage? Maggot-infested garbage? No way. I'm very selective. Somebody else can deal with that mess. Because I am not a servant of Waste Management, I am very, very picky.

Servants of Jesus Christ are not picky. Dealing with maggot-infested crud that's brought to the curb is not their favorite thing to do. Sometimes it really smells, but that comes with ministry. It's part of the assignment. Authentic servants of Jesus Christ just don't care a whole lot. And because they don't, it's easier for them to "blow it off."

"Men ought to regard us as . . . those entrusted with the secret things of God" (1 Cor. 4:1). Who are "those entrusted"? Think of an investment broker responsible for someone else's money or a flight attendant caring for the needs of his passengers—that is the idea behind the phrase. This is the second portrait in Paul's gallery. For the apostle, the entrusted assets—food of truth—were the "secret things of God" managed for his Master. Feeding God's household was an awesome responsibility, for which the cook dare not tinker with the assigned recipes. This was not Paul's own dinner to doctor up. Everything was God's—the food, the gifts to prepare the food, the know-how to serve

it in the right way at the right time to the right people. All of it was
from God. Because it was, Paul answered to Him, not to His critics.

Remember who your audience is. You live your life, use His spiritual gifts, serve as a servant, all before the audience of One. Your
ultimate accountability is to Him. He, and He alone, determines what
success is and what it's not.

This is not to imply people should not hold people accountable.
Quite the contrary. The Lord interposes individuals into our lives
who are commissioned by Him to hold us responsible within their
various spheres of influence. They are supervisors, teachers, pastors,
elders, deacons, board members, and those who serve in civil government to name a few.

But there are some who simply assume that role. They believe all
balance sheets—mistakes, no mistakes, bad work, good work, what's
said, what's not said—are due on their desk. There are others who
rightfully have oversight, but abuse it. They don't hold people accountable; they execute them.

When told by either the power usurper or the power abuser, "You
can't cut it," you must remember who ultimately makes cuts. If we do,
with Paul we can say, "I care very little if I am judged by you or by any
human court" (1 Cor. 4:3a). It's looking into God's gallery and seeing our portrait: one entrusted.

One of the worst ministry blunders you can make is to think you
are working for someone else.

- I work for the mission board.
- I work for the elder/deacon board.
- I work for the senior pastor.
- I work for the congregation.
- I work for a "para-church" ministry.
- I work for the denomination.
- I work for the school.

And the most deadly is the attitude of a spiritual entrepreneur: "I
work for myself."

No, you are a servant of the living God, and an unworthy servant
at that. You work for Him. God puts His servants in various places to

accomplish His purposes. Though we are to submit with positive attitudes and our very best effort for all those placed in proper authority
over us, it's from Him that we live to hear, "Well done."

What, then, is the point of coming unglued over unfounded criticism? Did you use your abilities loaned from above to carry out duties assigned to you by the Lord? Did you carry them out with a
passionate diligence? Have you been teachable? Are you still teachable? Are you still willing to be corrected if wrong or shown a better
way?

You said "Yes"? Then, friend, with graciousness, "blow it off."

KNOW THE STANDARD OF SUCCESS

I heard a story of a rancher who observed that when wolves attack
wild horses, the horses form a head-in circle and kick the wolves.
When wolves attack wild donkeys, the donkeys form a head-out circle
and kick themselves.

Spiritual wolves stalked the Corinthian church, and the congregation "hee-hawed." Like wild donkeys, the assembly ended up kicking
their own, including no less than the Apostle Paul himself. But there
were no resignations, no turning in his apostle's card, no giving up
the spiritual ghost. Paul survived. In the midst of the wild donkeys,
he rode high in the saddle of ministry.

That never would have happened if Paul had used his critics' paradigm for success: three-piece Oscar de la Renta suits and a BMW
parked in a five-car garage out in the suburbs on an eighteen-hole
golf course; first-class air travel between church consultant contracts.

Paul's suits were Salvation Army specials. He traveled on bunioned
feet. His only airline ticket was to heaven, one-way. Treated like a
criminal, he says,

> Five times I received from the Jews the forty lashes minus
> one. Three times I was beaten with rods, once I was stoned,
> three times I was shipwrecked, I spent a night and a day in
> the open sea, I have been constantly on the move. I have
> been in danger from rivers, in danger from bandits, in dan-
> ger from my own countrymen, in danger from Gentiles; in

danger in the city, in danger in the country, in danger at sea; and in danger from false brothers. I have labored and toiled and have often gone without sleep; I have known hunger and thirst and have often gone without food; I have been cold and naked.

—2 CORINTHIANS 11:24–27

No wonder the Corinthians rumored, "Failure." As they measured success, Paul was a fiasco. Their three-foot gallons, four-quart yardsticks, and twelve-inch liters proved it. This man was bargain-basement merchandise that was not going to move.

But Paul? No way would he use their mixed standards as a benchmark for success. A different criterion drove him: "Now it is required that those who have been given a trust must prove faithful" (1 Cor. 4:2).

Faithfulness. A three-foot yardstick . . . a four-quart gallon . . . a twelve-inch foot. That was what God used. That was what Paul used. And if you and I are sharp spiritually, that is the measure we will use, too. Faithfulness.

Bernie May, at the time director of Wycliffe Bible Translators, relayed the following in a letter to Wycliffe's constituents:

Dear Friends: I've never talked to anyone who knew they had just two weeks to live. But yesterday I sat down and talked to Dottie Weimer—who had just received that word from her doctor.

Dottie and her sister, Edie West, have been translators in Papua New Guinea for 20 years. Four years ago Dottie, who had been single all her life, married Harry Weimer, also a translator in Papua New Guinea. Harry's first wife had died of cancer after years on the mission field.

While Harry completed his translation with the Yareba tribe, Dottie and Edie continued work on the translation with the Ampeeli-Wojokeso people. They had just finished their translation and were doing the final checking when Dottie discovered she had cancer, too.

Several weeks ago Dottie flew back to the U.S. for additional treatment. But it was too late. The doctors said there was nothing they could do. Yesterday they told her she had but two weeks to live.

My wife, Nancy, and I went to visit her last night at the City of Hope Hospital near Pasadena. Despite her weakened condition, she lay on the hospital bed smiling . . . smiling . . . smiling. She had finished her task—almost. Edie had flown back to the States, at Dottie's request, so they could complete the final work on the New Testament. Dottie wanted to revise the book of Mark once again. God's Word, which she is leaving behind, must be perfectly translated.

Tonight, even as I write this, Dottie and Edie are putting the finishing touches on the book of Mark—working in the hospital room while Dottie's life slowly ebbs away. Then she will leave with the words of Jesus on her lips, "I have given them Thy word."

What a way to go![1]

Faithfulness. It's still doing your job when your surroundings scream, "Don't!" It is doing your job when everything about you says you are finished and when many others simply would not do it, period.

What matters is not to look happy. What matters is faithfulness. You have commitments to fulfill, and you fulfill them—whether savored or not, menial or monumental, a breeze or back breakers. You are faithful. You may be enthusiastic or maybe not; it doesn't matter. Faithfulness is faithfulness, whatever your disposition. You always do what you are supposed to do with all that you are. "But be sure to fear the LORD and serve him faithfully with all your heart" (1 Sam. 12:24a). From changing diapers to leading thousands, if you do it, you will do it right.

Assuming you are taking undeserved heat, now ask yourself, "Is my critic using faithfulness as the standard of success?" If the answer is *no*, I would be kind to the critic and not have a thing in the world to do with his criticism. Forget it. Ignore it. In one ear and out the other. Your critic knows not of what he speaks.

That's what Paul did. "I care very little if I am judged by you or by any human court" (1 Cor. 4:3a). That's not flippancy or an arrogant disregard for the personhood of the critic. It is a realistic assessment, based on what has taken place. Since the Corinthian critics did not use the right standard to make evaluations, those evaluations were invalid. So if they have no worth, why waste time and energy kneading them? Paul wouldn't. Listen as he continues to respond to the critical Corinthians: "I do not even judge myself" (1 Cor. 4:3b).

Paul was not against self-evaluation. Repeatedly, he reminded the Corinthians of a person's responsibility to examine himself. But when it was obvious the critics measured success by shoddy paradigms, Paul would have no part of it. He would not apply a rigged standard to himself.

"My conscience is clear" (1 Cor. 4:4a); something that always will be true when duties are faithfully discharged. Paul knew there was nothing like a mind and heart persuaded that all that could be done was done.

The standard is faithfulness, not super-pastor, super-speaker, super-leader, super-youth minister, super-staff person, super-brains. Faithfulness. And remember it does not always look like success.

The Bible says, "Moses was faithful in all God's house" (Heb. 3:2b). Several verses later Scripture emphasizes again, "Moses was faithful as a servant in all God's house" (v. 5a). Looking back, who would disagree? The man proved to be bigger than life! But as "faithful" Moses used his gifts almost 3500 years ago to lead his people through the wilderness, how many times did Israel try to run the guy out on a rail? The congregation repeatedly derided Moses. Listen to their sneers in Exodus 16: "If only we had died by the Lord's hand in Egypt! There we sat around pots of meat and ate all the food we wanted, but you have brought us out into this desert to starve this entire assembly to death" (v. 3).

To hear them talk, Moses had no vision. No sense of direction. He was inept. An absolute failure. But to heaven he was "faithful in all of God's house"—an outstanding success.

Faithfulness sometimes looks like success. We like that. We long for that. We can live for that. But sometimes faithfulness looks like outright failure. That's difficult. That's not what we prayed and fasted for. But, friend, it happens even to the Moseses, the Jeremiahs, and the Pauls. All failure is not faithfulness, but faithfulness is sometimes failure to human perspective, while to God it's a tremendous success!

Oswald Chambers said, "Watch where Jesus went. The one

dominant note in his life was to do his Father's will. His is not the way of wisdom or of success, but the way of faithfulness."[2]

If you are flying through flak, and faithfulness is not the standard, climb. Don't let yourself get emotionally shot down because someone else has targeted you a "zero."

KNOW WHO THE REAL CRITIC IS

Oprah Winfrey is reported to have said: "Lots of people want to ride with you in the limo, but what you want is someone who will take the bus with you when the limo breaks down."

Maybe you are on that bus now. It hasn't always been that way. There was a time in ministry when things were much better, but not now. With criticism hurled your way, you feel alone. Very alone. Possibly you are about to capitulate emotionally. That's where Paul was with the Corinthians, but he did not give in—and for good reason: "It is the Lord who judges me" (1 Cor. 4:4b).

You want a weight lifted off your soul? Remember that. When that day comes, your ump won't be your pastor, your elders, your deacons, your board, your charter members, or whoever else has said, "Strike one, strike two, strike three, you're out!" Say it to yourself. Say it out loud: "It is the Lord who judges me."

He knows the evidence—all of it. "Therefore judge nothing before the appointed time; wait till the Lord comes. He will bring to light what is hidden in darkness" (1 Cor. 4:5a).

Our Judge does not need witnesses to gather evidence or collect data through firsthand observation, procedures our critics must use. Our Judge simply *knows*—all that is, was, will be, could be, and could have been—and knows it without effort. He knows in your situation what is the truth and what is not—and always has known.

And the *know* is not just facts. He understands the "why" behind the facts. "He will bring to light what is hidden in darkness and will expose the motives of men's hearts" (1 Cor. 4:5b). Financier J. P. Morgan once commented, "A man always has two reasons for doing anything—a 'good' reason and a 'real' reason." As Judge of all, the Lord knows them both. "Deal with each man according to all he does, since you know his heart (for you alone know the hearts of all men)" (1 Kings 8:39b).

Maybe your critic knows some of the facts. Most likely he or she doesn't know them all, and what is known was gained either through personal observation or from someone else. That kind of judgment is pathetically inferior to that of our omniscient Father.

And our critics certainly lack the ability to examine motives. They see the outside, but never what goes on within. They don't hear your talks with the Lord and with yourself. Why then should you internally cower before a "so-called judge" who is obviously out of his or her league?

Paul didn't. "I care very little."

Neither should we.

He knows right and wrong. The One who judges us loves what is good and hates what is evil, loving and hating each with an absoluteness. He will not be persuaded otherwise. That's why Paul says in 1 Corinthians 4:5 that the Lord as judge "will expose the motives of men's hearts."

It's got to be that way because God is that way:

He is the Rock, his works are perfect,
and all his ways are just.

A faithful God who does no wrong,
upright and just is he.

—DEUTERONOMY 32:4

Your ways, O God, are holy.
What god is so great as our God?

—PSALM 77:13

Righteousness and justice are the foundation of your throne.

—PSALM 89:14A

The King is mighty, he loves justice.

—PSALM 99:4A

God is able to assess the evidence, knowing what price to put on each piece. He knows how to appraise what you did and what you did not do. All is ranked. Each piece is probed. Nothing is left unraveled.

He is the analyst's analyst. It's His nature: *fairness, equity, impartiality, objectivity, justice.*

Do those qualities describe your critic's make-up or your own? Who are we kidding. Both we and our critics are prone to shave the truth, to bias the facts, to show informational bigotry. Details are mispriced with some tagged too high and others being quite a steal.

But not God. He knows all the evidence, with each piece getting heaven's value.

Unintentional? "Price it according to ignorance."

Misunderstood? "Price it according to immaturity."

Intentional, but repentant? "Price it according to mercy."

> Therefore judge nothing before the appointed time; wait till the Lord comes. He will bring to light what is hidden in darkness and will expose the motives of men's hearts. At that time each will receive his praise from God.
>
> —1 CORINTHIANS 4:5

STICKS AND STONES

Vance Havner told the story of two gentlemen who stopped to look at a bird in the window of a taxidermist's shop. "That's sure a poor job of mounting a bird," said one of the men. Just then, the bird flew from the perch.

Belittled? Bad-mouthed? Roasted? Someone calling you a stuffed bird? You are not the first. They said it of the apostle Paul. The Corinthians considered the man a spiritual stiff, one ready for Ministerial Memorial Gardens—and then off his perch he flew! And so will you, if . . . and it's a big one . . . you embrace what Paul did:

- Know who you are: an entrusted servant.
- Know the standard of success: faithfulness.
- Know who the real critic is: your Lord.

If you do that, just wait. When your faultfinders least expect it, flap, flap, flap . . . another empty perch.

Chapter 6

WHEN TO TAKE A STAND

A wife stayed attentive to her husband's every need as he slipped in and out of consciousness. During one of those last "aware" moments, the man motioned for her to lean down: "You know, you've been with me through thick and thin. When I was fired, you were there. When the business flopped, you were there. When I was in the car accident and bills piled up for months, you were there. When the mortgage company foreclosed on our house, you were there. And now, as my health fails, you still stand with me. You know what?"

"What, dear?"

"I think you bring me bad luck."

Unjustified, off-the-wall criticism. We probably have all been guilty of giving it. For sure, we have all felt it, and it stung. It stung when you did your best, and still it's labeled slop; when you tried to do right, and still it's called wrong; when you meant for your presence to bless, and people talk like you are bad luck. Unjustified, off-the-wall criticism—how do you cope?

As seen in the previous chapter, if it's an ungrounded charge, you ignore it. We dispose of much unjustified, off-the-wall criticism as we do last week's garbage. Blow it off. Harry A. Ironside said, "If what they are saying about you is true, mend your ways. If it isn't true, forget it, and go on and serve the Lord."[1]

Great advice . . . most of the time. But there are exceptions. You and I cannot blow off all criticism as if it never happened. The writer of Ecclesiastes reminds us, "There is a time for everything, and a season for every activity under heaven" (Eccl. 3:1). That's another way of saying that every event has its own pigeonhole. Some things that you do in the morning, you don't do in the evening. Stuff you accomplish at the office you do not do at the mall. All that takes place in God's creation has a groove of its own, including "a time to be silent and a time to speak" (v. 7b). There is a time when it is necessary to take a stand, to deliver a defense, to give reason for your behavior motivated by the hope that resides within. There is just some criticism that you and I cannot afford to let slide.

On some occasions, Jesus ignored criticism. At other times, the Lamb roared. Stephen, in his early ministry, was commissioned to quietly serve the food needs of widows, for the most part a role with low-level criticism, if any. But in his closing ministry, when chided, Stephen said it like it was: "You stiff-necked people, with uncircumcised hearts and ears! You are just like your fathers: You always resist the Holy Spirit!" (Acts 7:51).

In his first recorded letter to the Corinthians, the Apostle Paul dismissed the church's kangaroo court: "I care very little if I am judged by you or by any human court" (1 Cor. 4:3a). But a short time later, to the same kangaroos he contended:

> I beg you that when I come I may not have to be as bold as I expect to be toward some people who think that we live by the standards of this world.
>
> —2 CORINTHIANS 10:2

> You are looking only on the surface of things. If anyone is confident that he belongs to Christ, he should consider again that we belong to Christ just as much as he.
>
> —2 CORINTHIANS 10:7

> For some say, "His letters are weighty and forceful, but in person he is unimpressive and his speaking amounts to nothing." Such people should realize that what we are in our letters when we are absent, we will be in our actions when we are present.
>
> —2 CORINTHIANS 10:10-11

But I do not think I am in the least inferior to those "super-apostles."

—2 CORINTHIANS 11:5

As surely as the truth of Christ is in me, nobody in the regions of Achaia will stop this boasting of mine.

—2 CORINTHIANS 11:10

I repeat: Let no one take me for a fool.

—2 CORINTHIANS 11:16A

Since many are boasting in the way the world does, I too will boast.

—2 CORINTHIANS 11:18

Are they Hebrews? So am I. Are they Israelites? So am I. Are they Abraham's descendants? So am I. Are they servants of Christ? (I am out of my mind to talk like this.) I am more.

—2 CORINTHIANS 11:22–23A

I ought to have been commended by you, for I am not in the least inferior to the "super-apostles," even though I am nothing.

—2 CORINTHIANS 12:11B

Enough was enough. Without question, Paul spoke in love, but that love thundered truth. For three chapters in his second recorded letter to the Corinthians (chs. 10–12), Paul passionately defended his ministry and calling. No apologies. No Mr. Nice Guy. No letting the church get away with it. *Now* Paul cared.

Why the reversal? Had the apostle been pushed emotionally over the brink? Was this really a fallen nature getting the best of the best?

No. Trepidation drummed Paul to words. Trepidation over how their criticism would reflect upon the Bridegroom, Christ: "I am jealous for you with a godly jealousy. I promised you to one husband, to Christ, so that I might present you as a pure virgin to him" (2 Cor. 11:2). Because the apostle had been instrumental in leading many at Corinth to the Lord, Paul viewed himself as a Middle-Eastern father who had arranged a wedding for his daughter (the Corinthians) to the Husband of all eternity, Christ. And he wanted his spiritual daughter to wait in purity for that wedding day so that Christ could have a pristine lady at His side (see Rev. 19:7).

But between engagement day (the day they trusted Christ as their Savior) and that coming wedding day (when Christ returns for His bride) some of the Corinthians had engaged in unjustified, disgraceful criticism of Paul (and other shameful behavior) that dishonored their husband-to-be. Christ's bride was fast becoming a loose woman. What a horrible reflection upon the Bridegroom of glory!

Paul also felt trepidation over what the criticism would do to the "bride," believers at Corinth. "I am afraid that just as Eve was deceived by the serpent's cunning, your minds may somehow be led astray from your sincere and pure devotion to Christ" (2 Cor. 11:3). With critical words laced with disgraceful behavior, the Corinthian church was in danger of walking out on Christ—a tragedy, especially for those in the church who had not yet bought into the grievous spirit of Paul's critics. Those still in the gray zone, unsure of what was going on with all this negative talk about the apostle, were at risk. The spiritual injury would be catastrophic. If things did not change, both hard-line critics and unsure noncritics would go the way of Eve— on the streets, eaten out of spiritual house and home. Critical words directed at Paul, mixed with sinful behavior, would seriously hurt the bride of Christ, and the Corinthians did not have a clue.

That was Paul. What about us? What if someone has impeached you with wrong:

- "You did not tell the truth at that meeting."
- "You are not doing what you are supposed to do."
- "You have been charging personal projects as ministry expenses."

But, it is not so. There is no way that it is so, but it's said as if it is. People with status make charges against you that will be believed by those who do not know better. Accusations have been slung. If not shot down, they have the potential to rip the heart out of a ministry. Because of your public identification with Christ as one of His servants, what is said reflects upon Him. No matter how you cut it, the spiritual damage could be serious. Do you handle situations like these as you would other criticism, or is this a time to defend yourself, to say, "Enough is enough"?

When unjust criticism libels Christ—given your public identification with Him and the likelihood of injury to others—the time has come to say, "Hold it. We need to talk." Trepidation forces us to talk. We fear how the criticism and its implications reflect upon the Bridegroom. We fear the criticism for its implications to the bride.

This is not an eye-for-an-eye or a tooth-for-a-tooth, barb-for-barb or dig-for-dig. That's self's calling card of retaliation. Instead, we are called to the Christlike response modeled by Paul, a lamb that, if forced to speak, will not stutter. It is the servant prototype, the kind that knows when to serve others with ears and when to serve them with words.

Let's look for a code of conduct that will help us stay Pauline when called to serve another with words.

MEEKNESS AND GENTLENESS

He was at it again. A leader in the church where I was pastor—let's call him "Frank"—was running me down before others. Of course I heard about it on the grapevine. (Don't we all.) I could live with the fact that Frank didn't like my sermons. After speaking, *I* sometimes didn't like my sermons. I could even live with the fact that he mocked them. But then to tell others that I had attempted to sabotage a rather significant ministry when I was the one who had spent untold hours initiating and mobilizing that ministry, encouraging those who served in it; to hear that I was reckless with my expense account, that I had already personally eaten double the amount allotted to me; to hear that I had never met with him to talk about his concerns when I had spent hours over the years doing just that. I heard it on the grapevine, and when I checked those grapes out, I found that Frank really had said these things—and then some. He had really turned missionary about me.

I decided to confront Frank head on. He lied. By my public identification with the Lord whom I loved, he insulted Him. He poisoned others against me. He made me look like a charlatan. That was it. No more.

"Either you cut it out, or I will nail your hide to the wall at the next board meeting. We will find out who's really been telling it like it is and who's telling it like it's not. We will find out who's lying."

That was the plan . . . pounded out on my pillow.

I'm glad I came to my senses and read how Paul handled his "Franks" in 2 Corinthians 10. There he lays out the spiritual parameters to any "take a stand" response: "By the meekness and gentleness of Christ, I appeal to you" (v. 1a). Paul could have argued his entire case with the very same words against his critics, without the "meekness and gentleness of Christ"—and grieved the heart of God.

Meekness. When my son Brian was in his single digits in age, I tussled with him on the floor and pinned him every time. But leave him black and blue with broken bones? Of course not. Power available is not power applied. To prevent harm I practiced restraint. That's meekness. Though power to do much harm is available—through information, money, position, knowledge, contacts—it's curbed. You could ruin your critic—it's all within your grasp—and you don't. Meekness waves a yellow flag and warns you to get out of the search-and-destroy mode.

Two millennia ago, our Lord could have blown away His pharisaical critics forever simply with a thought. Boom! But though the capacity was there, the will was not. Paul said to his critics concerning his authority, "[It is] for building you up rather than pulling you down" (2 Cor. 10:8).

Meekness cannot jerk another down. It is a short leash on vengeful desire. It is the safety lock on the automatic of bitter words. With meekness, you and I can take the heat of any situation and not torch our detractors into crispy critics. We practice restraint.

Gentleness. Quoting Isaiah 42:1-4, Matthew wrote of Christ, "He will not quarrel or cry out; no one will hear his voice in the streets. A bruised reed he will not break, and a smoldering wick he will not snuff out, till he leads justice to victory" (Matt. 12:19-20). That's gentleness: a sensitivity salved with mercy. When the time comes for "take a stand words," words that very likely will hurt, gentleness shrinks the potential pain as much as possible. Meekness is restraint: our words don't blow the critic away; gentleness is release: our words are spoken with sensitivity. The first handles the negative, the second handles the positive. Neither keeps us from saying what needs to be said; they keep us from saying too much.

Of course, some critics see meekness and gentleness as personal frailty. But unhealthy Christians and unbelievers cannot appreciate qualities that characterize spiritual maturity (see 1 Cor. 2:11–3:9). They look for what the world looks for: winning with clout. Not so for us, if we want to grow in our Lord. He values meekness and gentleness as parameters for any rationale for our behavior.

How do you feel toward your critic at this moment? Do you want to hurt him? Would you like to leave her broken and bent in shame? Or do you want to build your critic spiritually, hurting only as it is absolutely necessary? Would outsiders say that your proposed defense is gracious, or would they sense a vindictiveness?

Probing questions like these deserve honest answers before any defense is made. We must "by the meekness and gentleness of Christ" appeal to our critics.

NO-NO'S

But doing so in meekness and gentleness is not enough. There are some "no-no's." Paul defined his spiritual parameters by saying,

> For though we live in the world, we do not wage war as the world does. The weapons we fight with are not the weapons of the world. On the contrary, they have divine power to demolish strongholds.
>
> —2 CORINTHIANS 10:3–4

No to the world's techniques. Some in the Corinthian church charged Paul with "worldly living" because he no longer saw himself under the jurisdiction of the Mosaic law. The charge was fabricated by false apostles, out to undermine Paul's acceptance in Corinth. Indeed, he was no longer under the Mosaic law because he submitted to a higher law, the law of Christ. Though he lived in this sphere of fallen influences, he did not follow its methodology. "We do not wage war as the world does."

How does the world wage war? When defending itself, the world fights publicly—tearing the critic down in front of others. Not Paul. No gossiping to the Philippians: *"Do you know what they are saying about me in Corinth? 'Paul's really not an apostle.' Can you believe that, after all the miracles I've done? And they call themselves men and women of God!"* The Corinthian church, as carnal as it was, never became the butt of Paul's ridicule before other people.

When defending itself, the world wages war via campaigns—rallying support from others to fight for the cause. Not Paul. There were no church councils or gathering of sister congregations to rise up against the Corinthians. No circular letters to get people on his side. No politicking before the next Corinthian board meeting. No canvassing the church to find out whose side people were on. No plotting the next political move. None of that.

When defending itself, the world wages war against people—careless name calling that drags a person through the muck so that others will see the sludge and walk away from them, too. Not Paul. His criticism was oriented toward the issue, not the person. There was no sitting with a friend over a cup of coffee while alphabetizing all the Corinthians' defects. No roast pastor. No barbecued elder. No broiled deacon. No charred church.

None of those tactics. Paul rejected such strategies as the unprincipled policy of the world. "We do not wage war as the world does."

No to the world's arms. Hate. Spite. Malice. Ill will. Vindictiveness. Venom. Rancor. Resentment. Rage. Tantrums. Wrath. Provocation. Aggravation. Infuriation. Irritation. Jealousy. Snooping. Insolence. Cockiness. "The weapons we fight with are not the weapons of the world." When it came time to make a stand, none of that was for Paul.

It is tempting, though, to use those methods and weapons when savage criticism stings, is it not? The urge to bite back is strong. Forget about mercy and call fire down from heaven. Let's not kid ourselves: it is a titanic urge to secure ground with the world's schemes and ammo when hurt by unjust words. Yet Paul tells us to speak in meekness, with the gentleness of Christ. By doing so we save ourselves from unneeded stress.

A supervisor noticed a new man on the floor and instructed him to step into his office. "What's your name, son?"

"John," replied the new employee.

The supervisor bristled: "Hey, I don't know what kind of milk-toast outfit you came from, but we don't do that stuff here. On this floor I don't call anyone by their first name. It breeds familiarity that destroys lines of authority. Here it's last name only: Smith, Jones, Sanders. You got that? Now what's your name, son?"

"Darling," sighed the new guy. "My name is John Darling."

"Okay, John, the next thing I want to tell you is. . . ."

If you don't want to get yourself into a deeper hole when you've heard what you don't want to hear, value meekness and gentleness. Say "no" to this world's methods and weapons. To embrace those parameters is to squelch even more grief.

CORRECTLY USE AUTHORITY

But what do you do? If you have found it necessary to take a stand when criticized, what do you do in the way of a response?

For starters, whatever authority the Lord has given you, use it. Don't be sheepish. Paul had authority and was not self-conscious about using it. Read what he wrote to his critics:

> For even if I boast somewhat freely about the authority the Lord gave us for building you up rather than pulling you down, I will not be ashamed of it. I do not want to seem to be trying to frighten you with my letters. For some say, "His letters are weighty and forceful, but in person he is unimpressive and his speaking amounts to nothing." Such people should realize that what we are in our letters when we are absent, we will be in our actions when we are present.
>
> —2 CORINTHIANS 10:8–11

That's a man who knew how to use his authority. It came across loud and clear in his letters and would come across loud and clear on the church's front porch. With an authority inherent in the divine call to be an apostle, Paul would do whatever was necessary within the scope of his position to correct the prevalent wrong. When it came to living out his call, Paul was not embarrassed.

Are you a God-called leader? Are you being ground up by unjust criticism? Is the unjust criticism taking a toll on those you lead? Does it leave you looking as if you are a participant in willful sin? Then with meekness and gentleness make your defense. Do it without stooping for this world's methods and weapons.

> Don't have anything to do with foolish and stupid arguments, because you know they produce quarrels. And the Lord's servant must not quarrel; instead, he must be kind to everyone, able to teach, not resentful. Those who oppose him he must gently instruct, in the hope that God will grant them repentance leading them to a knowledge of the truth, and that they will come to their senses and escape from the trap of the devil, who has taken them captive to do his will.
>
> —2 TIMOTHY 2:23-26

I did confront Frank, but not in the way I pounded out on my pillow. Not too long afterward, I was caught off guard in a board meeting by his charges against me. Frank had gone from working the grapevine to CNN. This was a full-court press done for all the leadership to hear and see. The meeting crackled with electricity. If you don't know what I am talking about, thank the Lord. While Frank was speaking his mind with increased intensity, the Holy Spirit kept reminding me of what Paul said to Timothy: "For God did not give us a spirit of timidity, but a spirit of power, of love and of self-discipline" (2 Tim. 1:7). Rather than butt in and set him straight, God gave me grace to just let him talk. When he ran out of gas, guess who was front and center?

I defended myself without ripping his head off. I did not stutter, but I did not lose my cool. Within the providence of God, I was able to publicly refute Frank's allegations with facts that could easily be documented by the board. In fact, some who knew the truth of what I said spoke up to confirm just that.

I cannot say the Lord granted repentance leading Frank "to a knowledge of the truth." But I sure can say He granted it to me. If I had confronted Frank as I had wanted to confront Frank, there is no telling the bloody mess I would have made. God showed me by His

Spirit how to use my authority as a pastor with gentleness and meekness. Paul said to Titus: "Warn a divisive person once, and then warn him a second time. After that, have nothing to do with him. You may be sure that such a man is warped and sinful; he is self-condemned" (Titus 3:10–11). Since there was no indication of repentance, I was grateful that a second warning was not necessary. Frank left and moved to another church.

Don't be ashamed of your authority. Use it in a Christlike way. Stand up with gentleness and meekness for what is right.

STAY WITH THE FACTS

Because of the nature of unjust criticism, a defense will sometimes sound like boasting. And it may well be. Even that is all right if it's necessary to our defense *and done with integrity.*

> We, however, will not boast beyond proper limits, but will confine our boasting to the field God has assigned to us, a field that reaches even to you. We are not going too far in our boasting, as would be the case if we had not come to you, for we did get as far as you with the gospel of Christ. Neither do we go beyond our limits by boasting of work done by others. Our hope is that, as your faith continues to grow, our area of activity among you will greatly expand, so that we can preach the gospel in the regions beyond you. For we do not want to boast about work already done in another man's territory.
>
> —2 CORINTHIANS 10:13–16

Drug out of the closet and forced to speak, Paul had to do what he never wanted to do—stand up and say, "Hey, look at me." Boasting of one's own achievements has nil value (see 2 Cor. 12:1). But given the spiritual scene, it was something that had to be done.

Avoid it like the plague. But if the criticism is dead wrong, others do not defend you, and people are being misled, it may be necessary to state clearly what the Lord has allowed you to accomplish.

Say no more than what can be rightfully attributed to you.

Watch out for adjectives.

* "It was great!"
* "What a fantastic . . ."

Avoid putting words in people's mouths.

* "You would agree that . . ."
* "You would not have said or done anything different."

In his defense before the Corinthians, Paul was keenly conscious of the need to handle facts accurately, claiming, "As surely as the truth of Christ is in me . . ." (2 Cor. 11:10a), and "The God and Father of the Lord Jesus, who is to be praised forever, knows that I am not lying" (2 Cor. 11:31).

Exaggeration may sound good. It may seem to weight your argument more, but don't do it. Truth, not "truth and . . . ," is your best asset.

If you are put on the spot to declare what you've done, make sure what you say is verifiable. Keep to facts that can be documented by both sides. Paul said, "Even if I should choose to boast, I would not be a fool, because I would be speaking the truth. But I refrain, so no one will think more of me than is warranted by what I do or say" (2 Cor. 12:6). There were other facts to bolster his case, but Paul stopped short of sharing them. He wanted his critics to be able to document all that he placed on the table. What he called evidence, they, after examination, must call evidence.

That's tough. But we must learn to refrain from sharing things that our critic is unable to verify, even if we are certain it is true. Given the mind-set, especially if we sense a spirit of animosity, we must keep the defense to what our critic, too, *must* call facts.

USE YOUR LIABILITIES

Unless you are waiting to assume a vacancy in the Trinity, you know you have not arrived. You do have weaknesses, and very likely your critic has pinpointed some of them. Paul's critics did. Wisely, he referred to such in his defense and agreed, "I may not be a trained speaker . . ." (2 Cor. 11:6). Don't be afraid to acknowledge your liabilities. Refusal to do so says more about you than your critic. If the apostle could do it before his critical peers, so can we.

- "I know that is not one of my strengths."
- "What you said is true; I do have a difficult time with that."
- "I agree. It's never been easy for me to do it."

Agreeing with the critic about weaknesses does several things: First, it indicates that you are trying to make an honest evaluation of the criticism. If a person won't admit to personal weaknesses, then how can he or she fairly weigh others' remarks? For one whose critical remarks stem from ignorance, acknowledgment of weakness may open his ears to what we have to say.

Second, admitting faults gives a basis from which you can start your defense. That common ground gives a foundation for your side of the argument.

Third, it helps disarm your critics. If they know you intend to show them how wrong their charges are, what kind of audience will you have? Your critics will use that time to load the next salvo. They will be more convinced than ever that they were right. Why not catch them off guard? Agree with them on the points at which you can, especially those that focus on weaknesses you know you have.

Fourth, acknowledging weakness in a defense helps to maintain a proper tone in our response. It suppresses the electrical charges in the air—charges that could generate plenty of lightning and thunder. You don't want to end up in a shouting match.

In fact, Paul took what the Corinthians considered to be a terrible liability—the apostle's weaknesses—and demonstrated how they were really working to his advantage. Of one particular weakness, probably some physical disability, the apostle wrote:

Three times I pleaded with the Lord to take it away from me. But he said to me, "My grace is sufficient for you, for my power is made perfect in weakness." Therefore I will boast all the more gladly about my weaknesses, so that Christ's power may rest on me. That is why, for Christ's sake, I delight in weaknesses, in insults, in hardships, in persecutions, in difficulties. For when I am weak, then I am strong.

—2 CORINTHIANS 12:8-10

You and I can handle our weaknesses like that, too. And if the critic who has pointed out those things is a believer, share this exciting principle: "God is teaching me how He wants to more than compensate for the limitations I have."

Agree with your critic. Use your weaknesses in your response. That is one of the strongest elements in a godly defense.

DON'T FORGET YOUR AUDIENCE

Remember: Whatever your defense, the subject is going to come up again—before the Lord. That is why the apostle Paul said toward the close of his defense, "Have you been thinking all along that we have been defending ourselves to you? We have been speaking in the sight of God as those in Christ" (2 Cor. 12:19).

You and I need to remember that, too. Recalling who your real Audience is has a way of keeping self from erupting. It's like having your every thought and deed bugged:

You say it.
Your critic hears it.
God hears it.

You think it.
God hears it.

That should help keep us in check. If it doesn't, we have no business making a defense.

May I suggest a scriptural prayer request to add to your quiet time list? "Lead us not into temptation, but deliver us from evil." The Lord Himself told us to pray it—not just the words, but the resonance in those words. It is not a request begging our Father not to lead us into sin. That's impossible: "When tempted, no one should say, 'God is tempting me.' For God cannot be tempted by evil, nor does he tempt anyone; but each one is tempted when, by his own evil desire, he is dragged away and enticed" (James 1:13–14). Rather, it is a request for strength from one who feels his or her frailty. Like paper too close to fire, a Christian too close to the heat of a tempting situation may explode into flames. A "take-a-stand" response to criticism is just that sort of situation. This is a prayer of dependence for children of God who know their potential for wrong, crying out to their Father to keep them away from the flames.

"Lord, you know that what was said was not true. Lord, you know how deeply it cuts. Father, I fear what's inside of me. I do want to strike back. I do want to destroy. Lord, please don't take me down a path that will ignite old self. Lord, see to it that I make a defense at the right time using Your ways and weapons. If I cannot, I ask you to providentially hinder me."

The person who can pray that remembers who the real Audience is.

STRENGTHENING YOUR CRITIC

What is the ultimate reason for making a defense? To vindicate ourselves? No. If you have been wronged, God will take care of that in His time and way.

To show others the critic was wrong? If God's name is at stake, perhaps. That was part of the reason Paul argued his case before the Corinthians. A reflection upon him as God's called servant was a reflection upon God.

But Paul's primary motive was an enduring concern for the bride—including the part of Christ's bride that had turned on him.

> Have you been thinking all along that we have been defending ourselves to you? We have been speaking in the sight of God as those in Christ; and everything we do, dear friends, is for your strengthening.
>
> –2 CORINTHIANS 12:19

For their strengthening. That was why Paul took a stand. It was for the benefit of his critics. Wow! What a test to determine if our defense is of the Lord.

- Do we target our own need or our critic's need?
- Is our goal to nurture?
- Do we hope that the critic will be a better person?

Such questions get to the heart of the matter. They tell us quickly whether we speak in defense of truth or in defense of self. Self does not care what happens to the other person unless that person's well-being is linked to self's. Self could never answer these questions in the affirmative. Strengthen? Sure—to fatten the victim up for the kill!

But the maturing child of God wants to fatten the critic up for the kingdom. Maturity desires that the critic press toward that goal of Christlikeness by encouraging, motivating, developing, bettering, growing, bolstering in the faith. In other words, do what the Lord has done and still does for us—we, who once were His critics. If that's your goal, chances are you can safely make a stand.

Should that be so, may God give you the wisdom to know when, where, what, and how to say it. The Lord be with your spirit!

Chapter 7

WHEN SURVIVAL TECHNIQUES MAKE IT EASIER

Does it hurt?"

"What about now?"

"Do you feel it yet?"

Yes! But I couldn't tell him. His hands were in my mouth. It was an out-of-town emergency root canal, done by a butcher—I mean dentist—who reamed away. Shots. More shots. It did not matter. For some reason the tooth would not die. Nor would the doctor back off. Like a man on a mission to do what he had to do, he augured for big red.

"I won't be much longer."

He lied, too. With my muscles in a lock and palms in a fast sweat, my heart beat like a wild thing. He talked, but I did not hear. He gestured with his face, but I did not see. With that dentist and his chair, there was only one consuming desire—to get *OUT*.

ACT II

"We need to talk. What I have to say must be said, . . . and it must be said now."

And your critic says it . . . and says it . . . and says it.

Like a drill with a dull bit, tearing deeper and deeper, not satisfied until hitting big red. Muscles lock. Palms sweat. The heart beats wildly. Wave after wave of pain. Your emotional pulp lays bare, and still the critic just will not back off.

"This is for your own good."

And the tormentor lies, too. You hear words, but you don't hear words. You see a face, but you don't see a face. When will this be over? How much more of this can you take? And what about future appointments that you know have been booked? His words grind away, running up against raw nerve. He clamps. He picks. He chisels. He picks some more. Not appeased, he bores again. He's determined to get to the root of your problem.

And you? One thing and one thing alone consumes: You want *OUT.*

For some, that "out" comes through retaliation.

For miles and miles the two traveled, and not a word. Neither was about to concede ground in the argument back up the road. Passing a barnyard of pigs and mules, the wife finally sneered, "Relatives of yours?"

"Yep," the husband replied, "in-laws."

For some, that "out" comes through retaliation.

- "You're crazy!"
- "Let me tell you something!"
- "And you call yourself a Christian!"

Others cope with the pain through mental surrender. It is all a one-way street; rather than really take in what has been said, they automatically acquiesce. Finally, it's over. The criticized limps away, shredded.

In both cases, thoughts shove off unchecked. When that happens, things always feel worse than they really are. That is not to say what is said doesn't hurt. It most likely does. It is to say that too often we, through spiritual and mental unpreparedness, make it worse than it has to be, tormenting ourselves even more.

Now for a confession. After it was over, and the last appointment was history, I realized that my emergency root canal had been bad, but not *that* bad. I had survived. I always do when a dentist practices his trade between my jaws. But almost without fail, before the "after," I deadlock. Fear ripples into whitecaps. My glands dominate. Terror reigns.

It reigns, too, in our critic's examining chair. Because you did pick up this book, a fair assumption is that you've been racked by critics and may be racked again. You know there are more appointments. You know you will hear again the whine of their drill. If that is the case, may I suggest the following survival techniques to keep it from being worse than it has to be.

LAID BACK IN SPIRIT

U.S. bomber pilots during World War II had a saying: "Lose an engine and it's a long way home. Lose your head and it's a one-way trip." It's called panic, the stampede of fright, the very emotion to deflect when sitting in your critic's examining chair.

But how? Criticism usually catches us off guard. It is unexpected. If it weren't, we would either take evasive action or laser-bomb the critic right off the map. How do you relax when you've stumbled into significant flak?

"Cheryl, can we talk?" Of course they could talk, but she could tell by his tone of voice this was different. She could sense it by the way he looked at her. Static crackled. Okay, so she had not spent as much time ministering to the kids and their parents as she needed to, but there is only so much time.

She smells a verbal shellacking.

"Cheryl, we have got to talk. It's about you and the way you . . ."

Cheryl's mind bolts out of the gate. "He doesn't appreciate my abilities. He never has appreciated my abilities. I work. I work long hours. In fact, we would not have half the children's ministry we have now if it weren't for me. No, I know what the real problem is. He doesn't care for me. That's why he's so insensitive and loves these talk sessions. He treats me like one of his hired hands. He can go ahead and fire me. Maybe that's what all of this is leading up to . . . he wants to be done with me for good."

And with that, Cheryl doesn't hear another word. Both her heart and mind are whirling into a tailspin. She's on target for a spiritual crash and burn.

Avoidable? Without question. Cheryl ignored a truth that is the make-or-break for every believer. It is a truth that saw the Apostle Paul through many an attack. And when Timothy took the heat over his youthfulness and ways of ministering, Paul reminded him of it, too: "The Lord be with your spirit. Grace be with you" (2 Tim. 4:22).

The axiom: *No matter what you face, awareness of the Lord's presence and His grace will see you through. Where He is, His grace is. And where His grace is, the potential is there to handle anything.*

- Harsh words.
- Unfair words.
- True words.
- Stinging words.
- Abusive words.
- Insulting words.
- Damaging words.
- Provoking words.
- Annoying words.
- Crushing words.
- Exasperating words.
- Teasing words.
- Harassing words.
- Tormenting words.
- Infuriating words.

Grace is not an anesthetic. Neither is it a vaccination. Grace includes the ability to endure anything graciously. It is unmerited favor from the Lord that not only places us in His family but also grants us the capacity to always respond as one who resembles His family. And with His grace and presence, the skill is there to take whatever is slung our way.

To the Galatians Paul encouraged, "The grace of our Lord Jesus Christ be with your spirit, brothers. Amen" (Gal. 6:18). To the Philippians Paul penned, "The grace of the Lord Jesus Christ be with your spirit. Amen" (Phil. 4:23). To Philemon Paul said, "The grace of the Lord Jesus Christ be with your spirit" (Philem. 25). To Timothy Paul shared, "The Lord be with your spirit. Grace be with you" (2 Tim. 4:22). And what Paul reminded the Galatians, the Philippians, Philemon, and Timothy, by the Holy Spirit he reminds us: The Lord and His grace is with you and me. Amen.

Someone has said you might be a Baptist if you think:

1. John the Baptist started your denomination.
2. You are supposed to take a covered dish to heaven.
3. God's presence is strongest on the back three rows.

David says:

> Where can I go from your Spirit?
> Where can I flee from your presence?
>
> If I go up to the heavens, you are there;
> if I make my bed in the depths, you are there.
>
> If I rise on the wings of the dawn,
> if I settle on the far side of the sea,
>
> even there your hand will guide me,
> your right hand will hold me fast.
>
> —PSALM 139:7-10

It's not just the back three rows. God is everywhere as the omnipresent One. Through all time . . . through all space . . . through all infinity . . . through all eternity. He is not confined. He cannot be confined. And He is *fully present* through all time . . . through all space . . . through all infinity . . . through all eternity. Wherever God is, all of God is.

But when Paul tells Timothy (and you and me), "The Lord be with your spirit," and when he tells the Galatians, Philippians, and Philemon (and you and me), "The grace of the Lord Jesus Christ be with your spirit," the apostle is not talking about God as the omnipresent One.

He's talking about our Lord as the "relationship" One. This is friendship talk. Fellowship talk. This is one-on-one tenderness. He's talking about His unique love bond with us that He cherishes as He dwells within each of His own. In fact, as mentioned in a previous chapter, Paul makes a most profound statement about this unique love relationship when the apostle writes of those who have accepted Christ: "But he who unites himself with the Lord is one with him in spirit" (1 Cor. 6:17).

Wow! While you sit in your critic's "dental chair," it is that One who is with you in the most intimate way. And He says, "'Never will I leave you; never will I forsake you.' So we say with confidence, 'The Lord is my helper; I will not be afraid. What can man do to me?'" (Heb. 13:5b–6; cf. Deut. 31:6; Ps. 118:6–7).

Everything you experience in your critic's "dental chair," you experience in His presence:

- The shock.
- The disbelief.
- The confusion.
- The bewilderment.
- The hurt.
- The feelings of betrayal.
- The feelings of anger.
- The desire to strike back.

All of it, you experience in His presence. And if you are aware that He's there as you experience your "root canal," you will sense a check on doing the bad stuff (like blowing up your critic or mental surrender).

Instead, a consciousness of His presence helps you to relax. You are not feeling it alone. The psalmist said, "Even though I walk through the valley of the shadow of death, I will fear no evil, for you are with me" (Ps. 23:4). Paul wrote, "Rejoice in the Lord always. I will say it again: Rejoice! Let your gentleness be evident to all. The Lord is near. Do not be anxious about anything" (Phil. 4:4–6a). If you belong to the Lord, He is with you. He is near. His unique love-presence encompasses every thought, every feeling, every prayer, every word, every urge, every fear, every bit of it.

The axiom: *No matter what you face, awareness of the Lord's presence and His grace will see you through. Where He is, His grace is. And where His grace is, the potential is there to handle anything.*

When the first of each month comes, I face the greatest financial charge made against me: a mortgage payment on my house is due. If resources were not there, I would dread the first of each month. If I did not *know* resources were there I would dread the first of each month. Trepidation. Fear. But the Lord has been good. Come the first, the money has always been there, and I have known that it was there. When I have needed it, I have had it. Conscious of my resources, I relax.

Most likely you will make more trips to the chair. Charges will be made against you, possibly the greatest charges you have ever faced. If resources are not there to handle those charges, you will dread that chair. If resources are there to handle those charges, but you do not *know* they are there, you will dread that chair.

If you know the Lord, He has been good to you. Come each appointment in that chair, He has already seen to it that you have what you need to handle those charges in a way that reflects who you belong to. You have what you need for that moment . . . and the next moment . . . and the next moment. . . . If you know that, you will relax.

Know it. Realize now that the Lord is with your spirit. Realize that where He is, His grace is. Thank Him right now for that. And ask Him in advance to remind you of it the very moment you hear the shrieking whine of your critic's drill.

- "He's with me now."
- "His grace is sufficient for all that I am hearing."
- "I possess the spiritual capital."
- "I can handle what's facing me right now in a manner commensurate with my Lord."

Fear always stiffens. It deforms our perspective. We forget our spiritual assets. But when we remember "the Lord and His grace," we relax. He and His gift give us the ability to take things as they really are.

> But as for me, it is good to be near God.
> I have made the Sovereign LORD my refuge.
> I will tell of all your deeds.
>
> —PSALM 73:28

LAID BACK IN BODY

Remember Cheryl? Because she did not recall her spiritual assets when her supervisor tried to talk to her about her performance, another factor came into play: her body. It took charge. "A heart at peace gives life to the body" (Prov. 14:30a). A heart not at peace? You guessed it—the whole shebang is up for grabs. A breakneck pulse. Taut muscles. Adrenaline on the gush. Sopping palms.

That's bad. It's then the mind short-circuits. Rather than think with the head, we fret with our glands. And when the glands scream "Attack!" we make a kamikaze dive into anyone in sight.

As you recall Who is with you, take charge of your body. As soon as that quiet confidence takes the edge off your heart because you remembered Who is with you, encourage your body to calm down as well:

Consciously breathe slower. Just taking a few deep breaths *in* . . . *out* . . . *in* . . . *out* . . . gives the body a chance to cool off. It breaks the fight-flight cycle that tries to take hold when we feel assaulted. It gives the opportunity to emotionally regroup. It's not something that's just going to happen. It's something you must make happen.

In . . . *out* . . . *in* . . . *out* . . .

Assume a comfortable position. Place your body where it has support. When being criticized, sitting in a chair with proper posture is much better than standing. On your feet more of your muscles work. On your feet and criticized, they work overtime. When you're caught off guard, and it looks like your critic is loaded for bear, suggest the two of you sit down. If your critic won't and a chair is available, go ahead and sit down. You don't need to expend needless energy.

Call for a timeout. If criticism must be given, take it. But sometimes it's necessary first to call a "timeout." You are losing control, and you know it. You can feel yourself torque up. Ask for a ten-minute break. The goal is not to evade conflict but to regain composure. Walk out of the room, use the restroom, get something to drink, anything to break the pattern gripping your body. When you return for the second half, you will be surprised how much better you are able to handle what is dished out. This is especially important if you are in the presence of a person with the "gift" of giving . . . and giving . . . and giving. Whether what he or she says is called for or not, said in the right way or not, you will miss an opportunity to respond at your very best if you don't suggest, "Let's take a short break."

A believer who is criticized but is in touch with the Lord and relaxed will suffer fewer wounds, and, in time, even fewer scars. No longer is the critic seen as an assailant. The words, though possibly painful, are not deemed daggers. The criticized is not at the mercy of his or her emotions. Instead, there is a frame of mind to take what is given—whether true, partially true, or not true at all—and use it for its greatest good. Rather than seeing the criticism as destructive, the believer now looks at it as an opportunity to grow.

Take charge of your body.

EARS THAT HEAR

Assuming that you are now in a frame of mind where you can listen, listen. Don't interrupt. Let your critic have his or her say. She could be right on. He could be dead wrong. But you won't know which if you don't commit yourself to hearing with ears that hear. "He who answers before listening—that is his folly and his shame" (Prov. 18:13).

That's the temptation. You want to "butt in"; to set her straight; to never let him think that your silence gives consent. But speaking to show that you're right and she's wrong is to run in the face of some sound wisdom:

> When words are many, sin is not absent,
> but he who holds his tongue is wise.
> —PROVERBS 10:19

> A man who lacks judgment derides his neighbor,
> but a man of understanding holds his tongue.
> —PROVERBS 11:12

He who guards his lips guards his life,
but he who speaks rashly will come to ruin.

–PROVERBS 13:3

Even a fool is thought wise if he keeps silent,
and discerning if he holds his tongue.

–PROVERBS 17:28

Effective listening begins when we walk in our critic's shoes and honestly try to figure out where he or she is coming from. Don't just listen to what is said. Listen to how it is said.

- Is the person at ease?
- Do you sense anger?
- Are your critic's words loaded?
- Does your critic seem to be cutting you some slack?
- Is there a sense of grief on his or her part?

Try to feel what that person feels. It could very well tip you off as to why what's being said is being said. Maybe you just happen to be a convenient lightning rod. . . . Kaboom! . . . and the bolts of anger were never really intended for you or you alone. You were simply at the wrong place at the wrong time.

Maybe there is truth to what is being said, but the words conceal rather than clarify. You are told, "You leave it all for me to do." Probably you don't, but enough is said to indicate that the person you serve with feels as if he or she is getting the short end of the deal. Some adjustment is most likely needed. To understand what is meant in what is said, we must try to think our critic's thoughts.

But there is another facet to effective listening—one that requires adjustment in our own thinking. We must mentally allow our critic the possibility of being right. She may not be, and given our nature, we don't want her to be. But integrity articulates: "Hear this out; that possibility does exist." Otherwise, you will—if not verbally then in thought—ignore the issues. You won't hear the words. The matter is already black and white: You are right; she is wrong. Case closed. That is the mark of a spiritual blockhead.

> The way of a fool seems right to him,
> but a wise man listens to advice.
> —PROVERBS 12:15

> A fool finds no pleasure in understanding
> but delights in airing his own opinions.
> —PROVERBS 18:2

Don't personify intolerance with everything that's said. Give your undivided attention. Maintain eye contact. Generate warmth through facial expressions and gestures. Take mental notes. Maybe even real ones. Really try to appreciate, if not what is being said, at least the one who is saying it. Even if you consider the criticism coming from an "enemy"—love him or her. God says to. And remember: as believers, you and I possess the capacity to do so. It is part of the listening process. Hearing with ears that hear.

SCIENTIFIC INQUIRY

Ears that hear do not imply mouths that are mute. Good listening includes good questions.

- "If I understand you right, are you saying . . . ?"
- "Could you be a little more specific?"
- "I think I am hearing you. Is this what you mean?"
- "How long have you felt this way?"

Sportsmanlike questions by the criticized discharge static in the air. They tell your critic, "You are not being turned off; I'm interested in what you say."

Questions also assure that what is being said is what is being heard. Sometimes in restating the concerns it becomes clear that what the person intended to say is not what was said. As we are not always the best of listeners when criticized, critics are not always the best of communicators. On both sides, nerves beget nerves.

Questions help to distinguish fact from what was *thought* to be fact.

- "You said three o'clock? I am sorry. I thought it was at three thirty."
- "You mean it was to be done like this? I understood the other way."

When asking questions—or for that matter in any response—avoid defensiveness, as well as pontificating. Now is not the time to play pope.

> A gentle answer turns away wrath,
> but a harsh word stirs up anger.
>
> —PROVERBS 15:1

> The heart of the righteous weighs its answers,
> but the mouth of the wicked gushes evil.
>
> —PROVERBS 15:28

> A man of knowledge uses words with restraint,
> and a man of understanding is even-tempered.
>
> —PROVERBS 17:27

The point is this: when criticized, listen to your critic. Don't contradict up front. Don't turn him off. Hear her out. Ask nondefensive questions. That in itself may neutralize excess acid. Such an unexpected response puts your "friend" on notice that you are concerned with the issues. With your demeanor you communicate, "I still respect you as a person created in the image of God; even though you are causing me pain, you are important; you are loved."

YOU SAY "TOMATO," AND I SAY . . .

But there comes a time when you must respond to what has been said. When the Lord stated, "Blessed are the meek," He was not saying, "Happy are the wimps." Meekness is not discount carpet for your critic's feet. Meekness is power in restraint, a wild horse tamed and used for productive purposes. It's a measured response. You have listened; you have tried to ascertain all the facts; now in a controlled manner you must give a reply.

Several possibilities exist. Maybe you need more thinking space to mull over what has been said. Tell the person, *"It's going to take me a little time to digest all that you have told me; may I have some thinking time, and then we can talk about it again soon?"* And then do it. Don't fear examining yourself by what has been said. Take it before the Lord and ask Him to show you what truth is in it. Don't be surprised if there is more there than you would like to initially admit. Promptly get back to the person.

Maybe you need to clarify some false assumptions your critic made. Do it and do it kindly, but don't stutter. There is no reason to be ashamed of the truth if what has been said is not the truth.

Maybe what's said is right. Should that be so, and deep down you know, don't stall for time. Forget the smoke screen. Terminate all diversion tactics. Humble yourself by confessing the truth: *"You know, what you said really rings. I guess I just had not seen it that way before. What do you suggest I do about it?"* . . . and with that, you and your brother are working together on possible solutions.

Granted, some critics are not interested in hearing any other side of the story. They have made up their minds. As judge, jury, and executioner, they have no interest in reopening the case. You are wrong—dead wrong. All they want from you is a signed confession. And if that is the kind of person you are ministering to, one of two responses is in order:

> Do not answer a fool according to his folly,
> or you will be like him yourself.
> —PROVERBS 26:4

> Answer a fool according to his folly,
> or he will be wise in his own eyes.
> —PROVERBS 26:5

Both possibilities are from the book of Proverbs. The first Proverb warns us of an ever present danger: the drain. It's getting sucked down to your critic's level. There in her muck you sling her mud: ridicule, scoldings, denunciations, a communicated conviction: "I'm never wrong. . . . You are always wrong . . . not to mention worthless."

However, if you ignore the second Proverb, the critic mushrooms in conceit. She rides off into the sunset with a head rivaling the sun.

So how do you know which one to apply? If you are serving a closed-minded person, determine if what has been said is outright foolishness. Is it criticism based on notion rather than fact? If so, and if the person is not interested in hearing your response, graciously ignore what she says. That in itself is a greater response than any explanation made.

Does what your critic says *seem* factual, but it is not factual? Then without stooping into her muck, seek a way to state the facts as you know them. It may mean getting together with pen and paper. List what she says to be the facts. List what you know to be the facts. Compare the list. Without being inflammatory, communicate what you know of the truth. You may cause her to think twice before she pulls that stunt again on you or someone else. You may not. But you have done her the greatest favor possible in her state. You have rebuked her, "speaking the truth in love."

Finally, there is a truth that is worth all of the above and then some. It is stated in the Gospels at least three times, implying an audience more far-reaching than simply its first-century hearers. It is a truth that carries two assumptions:

1. What is said about you is wrong.
2. What is said about you stems from your identification with Christ and the resultant outworking of practical righteousness.

If you can answer "yes" to those two statements, then Jesus had you in mind when He stated:

> But when they arrest you, do not worry about what to say or how to say it. At that time you will be given what to say, for it will not be you speaking, but the Spirit of your Father speaking through you.
>
> —MATTHEW 10:19–20

> When you are arrested and brought to trial, do not worry beforehand about what to say. Just say whatever is given you

at the time, for it is not you speaking, but the Holy Spirit.
—MARK 13:11

But make up your mind not to worry beforehand how you will defend yourselves. For I will give you words and wisdom that none of your adversaries will be able to resist or contradict.
—LUKE 21:14-15

For most, criticism seldom leads to an arrest. There are usually no trials. But if impugned because of our identification with Christ and His righteousness, there is a promise: Whatever we need to say will be given to us at the appropriate moment. The way we need to say it will be given to us at the appropriate moment. So don't sweat it. God is not going to leave you holding the proverbial bag.

THE INEVITABLE

An elderly gentleman took his first airplane ride. After landing he said to the pilot, "Thanks for the two rides."

"Two rides?" asked the pilot. "You only had one."

"No sir, two," replied the gentleman. "My first and my last."

If you have ever been hurt badly by another's tongue, once is enough. Someone else can take that next trip. Another can sit in that chair. Save that piece of leather for other hides, but not yours.

But, yes, yours. And if you take ministry seriously, it will happen again, and, very likely, soon.

Prepare yourself. Know your strategy.

1. Remember Who is with you and His amazing grace.
2. Take charge of your body.
3. Really listen.
4. Ask questions.

Then should a response prove necessary, you'll find timely words at your disposal. Your reply may not mean much to your critic. But it will mean much to heaven, and, in time, it will mean much to you. You made it. You can live on. You survived your critic's "dental chair."

Chapter 8

WHEN PRIMED TO FIRE

Sick in bed, a chicken glared at a bowl of soup on a tray in front of him. "Quit complaining and eat it," his chicken friend quipped. "Number one, chicken soup is good for the flu, . . . and number two, it's nobody we know."[1]

But it *is* somebody we know. Diced, simmered, then ladled up as broth for another, it is somebody we know quite well. Cooked well done, the criticized is you.

With the edge of a switchblade, your critic's words stripped away emotional hide—soft, tender, emotional hide—and did it ever hurt. Maybe they were faithful wounds, words you really needed to hear. Your friend loved you enough to see to it that you did hear.

Or maybe they were unfaithful wounds. You didn't need to hear it, but your "friend" was intent on making sure you heard anyway. Either way, now you have to live with what was said.

When you sip your breakfast coffee, those barbed words sip with you. When you run your errands, those same words come along. When you grab a midday bite, those words see to it that you don't eat by yourself. When you take mental work breaks, those very same words offer you an emotional massage. When you relax in the evening in your recliner, you don't relax alone. Come bedtime, they want to chit-chat. Come 3 A.M., they want you to get up to get a start on the day.

Like it or not, you now wine and dine an uninvited guest who feels at home and has every intention of staying.

You wish your guest would pack his bags and disappear; the memory those words dredge up is colossal in pain. Other times, strangely enough, you are glad your company is there. In fact, at times it seems as if you could not live without them.

That's just what those words wanted: for you to tuck them in and kiss them good night, and then wake them again when you start a new day. More than anything, those words want to be wanted as a friend. An intimate. One that you long to spend every free moment with.

Now you have a backer, a cheerleader, a confidante who can teach you much about criticism:

- How to do it.
- How to do it to your critic.
- How to do it to others.
- How to do it with little effort.
- How to do it without personal pain.
- How to do it without much thought.

Taught well and often learned well, it's second nature. Now you can take another person apart. Whittle him up in no time. You pinpoint shortcomings that others miss. You quickly pick up aberrations that friends do not notice. Like a heat-seeking missile, you can home in on the defects. Just mention the name, and you know precisely the coordinates for the flaw. Taught well and learned well, you don't miss a thing.

DETOUR

What has happened?

We are doing unto others as they have done unto us, and then some. We have taken to heart the admonition that it is better to give than to receive. The criticized has become the critic, the judged, the judge.

That is dangerous . . . very, very, dangerous. We have set up a spiritual chain of events that in the end—short of the mercies of God—will prove worse than any havoc caused by another's critical words.

It's a repercussion the criticized are often unaware of. When painful words impale us, true or not, we enter a high-risk zone, one that has a phenomenal casualty rate. Unless checked, our once innocent thoughts turn malignant. Our once benign words run wild. And in no time, we process our critic like paper in a shredder. As judge, we deliver the verdict: "Condemned. Case closed."

Really closed?

Not quite.

> Do not judge, or you too will be judged. For in the same way you judge others, you will be judged, and with the measure you use, it will be measured to you.
>
> Why do you look at the speck of sawdust in your brother's eye and pay no attention to the plank in your own eye? How can you say to your brother, "Let me take the speck out of your eye," when all the time there is a plank in your own eye? You hypocrite, first take the plank out of your own eye, and then you will see clearly to remove the speck from your brother's eye.
>
> —MATTHEW 7:1-5

The Lord said that. It's a barricade, not so much for the person who has turned hypercritical—he has already smashed through the flashing roadblocks. Once criticism revs up, it's hard to stop. Once over the cliff, it's somewhat difficult to reverse the trend.

No, these words are a roadblock designed for one passing down the highway that leads to a critical spirit.

Case in point: A criticized you, and you are ready to let fly. Your critic has torn into you, and now, armed, you are primed to fire. Doing so seems right. What's good for one is good for the other.

But the Lord's words in Matthew 7 lie right in the middle of the thoroughfare, a barrier meant to detour us to the safe way. It's a warning and a full explanation of the reason for the warning. It shows both how and how not to criticize. To ignore these words when you are ready to let rip is to ignore inevitable, unavoidable, decreed consequences you never dreamed of.

Once criticized by another, it's time to take to heart the Lord's alerts in Matthew 7.

WHAT IS JUDGING?

First things first. If we say something construed as negative about someone else, have we judged? Have we just done what the Lord says not to do?

A college-aged friend of our family recently interned for twelve weeks with the Federal Bureau of Investigation, a national policing agency for the United States. Specifically, he was placed with the Electronic Surveillance Technologies Unit in the Bureau's engineering research facility in Quantico, Virginia. He shared with us that the unit's motto is *"In God we trust. All others we monitor."*

You are criticized by a person who frequently criticizes others . . . and you say so. Your critic is not well versed in the subject area of the criticism . . . and you say so. Your critic refuses to listen to your explanation. It's obvious he is convinced he is right and always right . . . and you say so. Your critic cannot speak without venting his spleen . . . and you say so.

Have you turned FBI? You trust in God, but all others, especially your critic, you monitor? By "saying so," have you done what Jesus said not to do—"Do not judge, or you too will be judged"? If that's the case, then Paul turned FBI too:

> Even though I am not physically present, I am with you in spirit. And I have already passed judgment on the one who did this, just as if I were present. When you are assembled in the name of our Lord Jesus and I am with you in spirit, and the power of our Lord Jesus is present, hand this man over to Satan, so that the sinful nature may be destroyed and his spirit saved on the day of the Lord.
>
> —1 CORINTHIANS 5:3-5

Wow. Paul "said so," and he did not stutter.

Or what about what John wrote in his first epistle? If this is not FBI stuff, what is?

Dear friends, do not believe every spirit, but test the spirits
to see whether they are from God, because many false proph-
ets have gone out into the world.

—1 JOHN 4:1

Is that not judging?

It is, and it's okay. We are to discriminate between true and false
servants. Like Paul, we are to call bad behavior "bad" and good behavior "good." Jesus himself said, "Stop judging by mere appearances,
and make a right judgment" (John 7:24). There is a place for judging,
which means something is out of balance when we hear Matthew 7:1
cited as proof that we are not to judge. It's pitting Scripture against
Scripture and declaring only one the winner.

When Jesus said, "Do not judge, or you too will be judged," this
was not a command to unscrew our heads. The concern is not over
making any judgment but over being judgmental. It's officiating your
neighbor's every move, and that includes every move of those you
serve. It's the verbal ump squatting behind every opportunity to shout,
"You're out." It's respect that has lost out to utter contempt.

- "Why can't she ever get here on time?"
- "What's her I.Q., anyway?"
- "And he calls himself a deacon!"
- "You're joking. Tell me you are joking."
- "My four-year-old could lead that ministry better than he does."

Derogatory in our remarks. Viciously attacking the personhood of
the person. Ridiculing him before his peers. As if we can see into his
heart, blowing the whistle on his motive. In a fit of humility, we are
persuaded the criticized has met his judge, and it is us.

And ministry is where it seems to happen the most.

AN ABSOLUTE ESSENTIAL

"Flight 854," the control tower advised, "turn right 45 degrees for
noise abatement." "Roger," answered the pilot, "but we're at 35,000
feet. How much noise can we make up here?"

"Sir," said the controller, "have you ever heard the noise a Lear Jet makes when it hits a 747?"

Friend, once we flirt with vigilante justice, it's absolutely essential we turn "right" for noise abatement. Otherwise, you and I will hear a boom, the likes of which we have not heard before. "Do not judge, or you too will be judged" (Matt. 7:1).

What makes this so sobering is the One who said it. His is not a condemning disposition. This is no security guard twirling his night-stick, ready to show his stuff. This is the most merciful God, full of grace, the very definition of patience. And without hesitation He says, "Do not judge, or you too will be judged."

By whom? The answer is not stated, but certainly implied. "For we know him who said, 'It is mine to avenge; I will repay,' and again, 'The Lord will judge his people'" (Heb. 10:30). The Magistrate is God.

How? The mode also is unstated. But where there is a judgment, there is a sentence. It may be very direct, or He may choose to use other people, in particular, critical people. The believer's eternal status is not in question; Romans 8:1 and other passages make that clear. The judgment of Matthew 7:1 for the Christian involves a loving Father's disciplining hand.

When? That we do not know either. Maybe right on the heels of the criticism. Maybe much later. The time is set by Him.

Where? Again, that is up to the Lord. Our humiliation may be seen by those we condemned. It may occur out of sight. On this earth, or at the judgment seat. There will come a time when judgment comes crashing in on our foolish heads.

This warning in the Book is meant for all, in particular, God's children: "Do not judge, or you too will be judged." Only the fool-ish ignore it. If we choose to dish it out, we are going to lick the dish.

JUDGED: HOW?

Of the "Who? How? When? Where?" questions, the Lord devotes most attention to the "how?" Though not specific with names or set-tings, He does let us in on how it will happen to the one who has turned critical: "For in the same way you judge others, you will be judged" (Matt. 7:2). Possibly different faces, a different set of circumstances, but without question done in the same way.

What is your emotional rapport toward the one whose words make life uncomfortable for you? Is "merciful" a stretch of the imagination? Do you peruse his life with a magnifying glass? A microscope? Are you trash hunting? How would you feel if you hit pay dirt, a real gold mine of muck? Would you be glad?

Deep down, would you shout "Party time!"?

What about that ever-present urge to share that good news with others, like your peers in ministry or close friends—would you do it? "Look what I found. Isn't that just terrible?" Would it become an obsession? Every time the subject of ministry surfaces, would you turn anchorman? "Good evening. CNN has learned that . . ." Would you broadcast the truth you found?

If that is more or less where you are now, read again our Lord's words: "For in the same way you judge others, you will be judged." Maybe different faces, possibly different circumstances, but in the same way. There are no footnotes. No qualifying statements. No exception clauses to exclude certain classes of Christians. This is one of those blanket statements that covers us all. You do it; you get it. The way we handle our critic—and anyone else for that matter—is the way God will see that you and I are handled. It's one of those gravity laws in His moral handbook that has no switch to click off.

Jean just cannot understand why her young adult children will have nothing to do with her. As a Christian servant, she poured her life into them, even homeschooled both of them, and they want nothing to do with Mom. And they tell her to her face. Critical of her. Hyperhypercritical of her. You name it; no matter what Jean does, the two find fault. She just does not understand.

What she really doesn't understand is this: "For in the same way you judge others, you will be judged." For years Jean tore down the one who God called her first to serve—her husband. Hypercritical of him, no matter what Jim did, she found fault. It's one of those gravity laws in God's moral handbook that has no switch to click off.

Most things you and I do, we do without giving the force of gravity much thought. It is there. It operates around the clock. Whether in bed, behind the wheel, or on our feet, gravity just is. We simply make sure we engage in activities that have no built-in repercussions.

Likewise with this spiritual law. It, too, is there. Always there. When we are tired. When we've been hurt. When we are criticized. When we are enraged. Our Lord's pronouncement, "For in the same way you judge others, you will be judged," just is. The wise servant learns to engage in activities that have no built-in repercussions.

To rough up your critic or anyone else is to rough up yourself. To inflict needless pain with your words is to paint a bull's-eye on your back. To mishandle the truth in order to score against the one who has scored against you is to get slam-dunked.

"So, Blaine," you may be thinking, "the reason I'm now criticized is because I criticized?"

Maybe. Maybe not. When you start working backward from principles like this one in Matthew 7:2, you can reach all kinds of flawed deductions. However, it is a warning to now choose mercy. If we mercilessly lay into our critic because of what he or she has done to us, we are booking our own judgment—one that likewise will run low on mercy.

"But, Blaine, you don't know what they have done to me and my family. None of them deserve mercy," you argue.

You are right. They don't. Mercy is not mercy if it is deserved. Mercy is for those who do not deserve it, which, by the way, includes you and me.

And besides, if we show mercy to others, God—though He is not obligated no matter how merciful we are—has chosen to show mercy to us. Remember that beatitude, "Blessed are the merciful, for they will be shown mercy" (Matt. 5:7)? It's the flip side of the Matthew 7:2 principle: If we show mercy to others, including those whose words lacerate us, mercy will be shown to us—by God and by those He brings into our lives. With grateful hearts, we will say "thank you" for the warm hand of mercy offered to us.

JUDGED: WHAT STANDARD?

But there's more: "For in the same way you judge others, you will be judged, and with the measure you use, it will be measured to you" (Matt. 7:2).

- "He shouldn't be doing that."
- "She knows better."
- "I would never say a thing like that."

Statements like these assume a personal standard: We know the "shoulds." We are aware of the "betters." The "nevers" we are well acquainted with. The yardstick of values used for others is proof we are knowledgeable of them ourselves.

Statements like these also assume that the one using those criteria measures up himself—inconsistencies criticized in the life of another are not in our own. When we actively dig for dirt in others, we are saying our life is as pure as the driven snow.

So what does the Lord warn us of? The standard we administer will be administered to us.

"She does not tell me what's really going on." That means somewhere along the way we realized it is right to tell the truth to others. Truth all the time, never shaved. The same ruler will measure us.

"He does not pull his fair share in the ministry." Our application of the straightedge called fairness—a good gauge—says we know what fairness is. It will be applied to us and what we do.

"She will not let me forget my mistakes." The implication is that we know the importance of forgiving others. It's a good standard. And because we have light in that area, we, too, will be measured by it. Do you forgive others—including your critic?

"He really never shows love. He is so cold and stiff." In other words, you know how to love your critic because you know the law of love, a good standard.

It is dangerous to say, "I know the standard." But that is exactly what we are saying when we choose to criticize the shortcomings of someone else. In that given area, we know the truth; our criticism is a dead give-away. The Lord's reminder: "With the measure you use, it will be measured to you." It's judgment based on the light that we have. You cannot get any more ethical than that.

WHAT SHOULD BE DONE?

Maybe you heard about the sign tacked up in front of a convent:

"ABSOLUTELY NO TRESPASSING—VIOLATORS WILL BE PROS-
ECUTED TO THE FULL EXTENT OF THE LAW. The Sisters of
Mercy."

Oswald Chambers said, "We are going to meet unmerciful good
people and unmerciful bad people, unmerciful institutions, unmerciful organizations, and we shall have to go through the discipline of
being merciful to the merciless."[2]

Mercy. That's the stance to take when criticized. No matter what
has been said, you and I are to cut our critics slack. Give them what
they do not deserve: kindness, respect, understanding, consideration.
In the midst of it all, share with others a good word about some
beneficial trait in their life. Give them your time. Give them your ear.
Give them yourself.

And if there really is an issue that your critic needs help with—a
particle in the eye?—the Lord tells us what to do:

> Why do you look at the speck of sawdust in your brother's
> eye and pay no attention to the plank in your own eye? How
> can you say to your brother, "Let me take the speck out of
> your eye," when all the time there is a plank in your own eye?
> You hypocrite, first take the plank out of your own eye, and
> then you will see clearly to remove the speck from your
> brother's eye.
>
> —MATTHEW 7:3–5

Check yourself first. It was inspection time, and all was going well
until the colonel came to a soldier who had missed a detail on his
uniform. The officer stopped, looked the young man in the eye and
barked, "Soldier, button that pocket."

"Now, sir?"

"What kind of question is that? Of course, now!"

The soldier, with extreme care, reached over, and buttoned the
colonel's pocket.

The person who has become critical focuses on relatively minor
concerns in others. It's not that they are not legitimate matters; very
likely, they are concerns that do not measure up to God's standard,
which, by the way, is one of perfection. However, they are minor in

comparison with the critic's own failings. The Lord said, "Why do you look at the speck of sawdust in your brother's eye and pay no attention to the plank in your own eye?" (Matt. 7:3).

The critic combs for that particle of sawdust. He drains hours of time and energy just to get a flaw out in the open. But in doing so, he has ignored the two-by-four that's in his own eye. Finding a sin in a brother, he ignores greater sin in himself. That's what pride does. It blinds us to our own faults, even as we critique our neighbors.

Have you discovered any faults in yourself recently? That is an excellent test to determine if what you are saying about those critical of you is really judging in the bad sense. The hypercritical person sees few—if any—of his own failures.

Do you pray, "And Lord, if I have sinned, I am sorry," as if personal sin is theologically possible but highly unlikely? Or do you find yourself calling out sins by name before the Lord? Regularly? A hypercritical person is often theologically correct, knowing that believers commit sin; but pride assumes that for him it is not really so. He attacks his brother for the pinch of sawdust in his eye. He really gets critical. Error is judged. But the plank in his own eye?

What plank?

Before you tell your critic to button his pocket, you had better check your own.

Correct yourself first. Once the hypercritical person finds that grain of sawdust in someone else's eye, he cannot live with himself unless something is done. Something is—and is it ever a mess. "How can you say to your brother, 'Let me take the speck out of your eye,' when all the time there is a plank in your own eye?" (Matt. 7:4).

Eye surgery is risky. You need patience, gentleness, and good vision—none of which the hypercritical person possesses. He wants to get that speck out, and he wants to get it out *now.* Whatever it takes to extract it, the butcher will do—leaving a ministry emotionally bloodied, a volunteer blinded with anger, a once troubled church massacred.

Friend, the plank must go. Deal brutally with yourself first.

Since both the plank and sawdust in essence are wood, don't be surprised that the sin you are now so committed to dislodging in your critic is in yourself, too.

Irritated with the hacking cough of her pet macaw, a lady took her bird to the vet. After an exam and tests, the vet concluded: "Nothing is wrong with this bird. He's just imitating what he hears." A chain smoker, the lady had a chronic, hacking cough.

Is it your critic's closed-mindedness that has ticked you off? Guess what? Is it his temper that has gotten under your skin? Guess what? The speck of sawdust in his eye is but a hint of the log that's in your own. Friend, the plank must go.

And how is it to be removed? Repentance. Confession. Restitution. That is the only way to yank girders out.

"God opposes the proud
but gives grace to the humble."

Submit yourselves, then, to God. Resist the devil, and he will flee from you. Come near to God and he will come near to you. Wash your hands, you sinners, and purify your hearts, you double-minded. Grieve, mourn and wail. Change your laughter to mourning and your joy to gloom. Humble yourselves before the Lord, and he will lift you up.

–JAMES 4:6–10

Wash and make yourselves clean.
Take your evil deeds
out of my sight!

Stop doing wrong,
learn to do right!

Seek justice,
encourage the oppressed.

Defend the cause of the fatherless,
plead the case of the widow.

"Come now, let us reason together,"
says the LORD.

"Though your sins are like scarlet,
they shall be as white as snow;

though they are red as crimson,
they shall be like wool.

If you are willing and obedient,
you will eat the best from the land;

but if you resist and rebel,
you will be devoured by the sword."
For the mouth of the Lord has spoken.
                                    —ISAIAH 1:16–20

How is the beam removed? Repentance. Confession. Restitution.
That is the only way to yank girders out.

NOW WHAT?

A little seed lay on the ground,
And soon began to sprout.
"Now, which of all the flowers around,"
It mused, "shall I come out?

The lily's face is fair and proud,
But just a trifle cold;
The rose, I think, is rather loud,
And then, its fashion's old.

The violet is all very well,
But not a flower I'd choose;
Nor yet the Canterbury bell
I never cared for blues."

And so it criticized each flower,
This supercilious seed,

Until it woke one summer morn,
And found itself a weed.[3]

Is that what you want to be? Do you want to wake up later in your
ministry, in your marriage, later with your children, later in your life,
and find yourself a weed?

That's what you will become if you don't show patience toward
others, starting with your critics—yes, those you have served who have
hurt you with their critical actions and tongues.

Are you forbearing with people in your ministry? Whatever you
see in your critic's spiritual eye, do you understand the absolute necessity of gentleness in any kind of contact with that eye? Do you
regularly check your own eyes before you start toward another's?

The One who has the right to judge does not hesitate to judge the
person who refuses to ask such probing questions: "You hypocrite,"
He says (Matt. 7:5). *Hypocritēs* was a word used for actors, people who
perform one way on stage and another in real life. Acting is fine if
everyone knows you are doing it. But hypocrites? They think they are
for real. Self deceived, they believe the part being played: "I do live
up to the standard I am measuring you by; I am the model for this
ministry."

Be different. If the urge strikes to play surgeon, play it safe. Assume there is a plank in your own eye. You become the patient. "Physician, heal thyself."

Your critic may have been in the wrong.

You may know things about him that are wrong.

But now you hurt for him. You feel compassion. You pick up the
scalpel only out of a deep sense of necessity—and pain.

You remember the warning:

Why do you look at the speck of sawdust in your brother's eye
and pay no attention to the plank in your own eye? How can
you say to your brother, "Let me take the speck out of your eye,"
when all the time there is a plank in your own eye? You hypocrite, first take the plank out of your own eye, and then you will
see clearly to remove the speck from your brother's eye.
—MATTHEW 7:3–5

Chapter 9

WHEN AN EXPLOSION SEEMS INEVITABLE

How are you feeling, dear?" asked a church member who was visiting a ninety-five-year-old woman in the nursing home.

"Oh, I'm just worried sick."

"What are you worried about?" asked her friend. "Are they treating you well? Are they taking care of you?"

"Yes, they are taking very good care of me."

"Are you in any pain?"

"No. I haven't felt this good in months."

"Well, dear," asked the friend, "what are you worried about?"

The lady leaned forward in her rocking chair and confided: "All my friends have died and gone on to heaven. I'm afraid they all wonder where I went."[1]

Relationships. They are important, are they not? We don't want people to think badly of us. And we should not want to think badly of them. Even when a relationship is strained, there should be something in us that wants it to be right. Abraham Lincoln is reported to have said, "No matter how much cats fight, there always seem to be plenty of kittens."

But what if the fight will not stop? What if there are not plenty of kittens?

"We have been married fifteen years and haven't agreed on a thing," blared a husband to his wife. With ice in her voice, she chilled, "That's not so. . . . It's been sixteen years."

What if there is not even a hope for kittens?

With some, there is just no living on the same page. Every word is a gunshot. Every conversation a fray. You've been wounded time and time again. Things have been said that never should have been said, attitudes vented that soiled the air.

And it's just getting worse. The tension has pitched to such a level that the battered relationship is about to blow. It's a time bomb. You are not sure when it will go off, but chances are it won't be long. If nothing is done, the outcome is predictable. You and the one you thought you were there to serve are destined for a blast that will blow the relationship to shreds. Do nothing, and it's inevitable.

tick . . .

tick . . .

tick. . . .

You hear it. It gets louder. No question, it's going to blow. But your critic doesn't hear it. He doesn't realize what is taking place. Caught up in his criticism—whether legitimate or not—he's unaware that the relationship is on the line. If it goes, the boom could be for good. All over. Finished.

Possibly the one slinging words your way doesn't even care, but you should. If you belong to the Lord, you should exercise everything in your power to prevent the relationship from going up in smoke. And that is doubly so if your critic is a brother or sister in the Lord. You are family.

tick . . .

tick . . .

tick. . . .

No doubt it is tough to both take the criticism and, in the midst of the heat, nurture the relationship. Especially given those weaker moments when you don't care. But it's in the believer's job description: "If it is possible, as far as it depends on you, live at peace with everyone" (Rom. 12:18).

Of course it takes two to tango. If your critic spoke not to aid the situation but to prove his way was right no matter what, then there is not a whole lot you can do. If he insists on dancing with nitroglycerine, there is no way he can juggle the bottles for long. One slip and . . .

But we are still to try: "If it is possible, as far as it depends on you . . ." Paul said. We, the criticized, are to show the kind of maturity that looks beyond what is said; that sees further than time; that knows at eternity's judgment seat we will give account for this very hour. The Lord does not say through Paul's pen, "Live in peace with all, no matter what"; rather, He qualifies His charge: "If it is possible" and "as far as it depends on you."

tick . . .

tick . . .

tick . . .

With the one you've been called to serve on the other side of that "tick," *you* are the one who recognizes the bomb. For the sake of your neighbor, yourself, whoever else is in the area—and the Lord—you must do your best to defuse it.

The following are "bomb squad" techniques that have worked for others.

THE REST OF THE STORY

New at the monastery, an inquisitive monk asked why the brothers were copying from copies and not from the original books. The newcomer pointed out to the head monk that an error in the first copy would appear in every copy afterward.

"We've been copying from copies for centuries, my son, but you do make a good point," and with that the head monk took the newest copies and headed down to the cellar to check them against the centuries-old originals.

Not heard from for some time, another monk headed down to search for him. He found the head monk in the corner, stooped over the original, sobbing, "The word is 'celebrate,' not 'celibate.' . . ."[2]

Truth, the whole truth . . . when it comes too late, the tears can flow. When things that are not altogether true are communicated again and again, it can leave both parties in a pool of regret. As suggested in a previous chapter, determine to get "the rest of the story" up front.

People who get the rest of the story up front listen inquisitively.

They put pieces together. They try to find out quickly where their critic is coming from. Ask Peter. He was dumped on, and not just by unbelievers.

> The apostles and the brothers throughout Judea heard that the Gentiles also had received the word of God. So when Peter went up to Jerusalem, the circumcised believers criticized him and said, "You went into the house of uncircumcised men and ate with them."
>
> —ACTS 11:1–3

Peter was raked over the coals by Jewish believers because he did what no good, self-respecting, God-fearing Jew would ever do: schmooze with the Gentiles. These were his friends. Peter was their leader. As a fisher of men, he had only done what Christ wanted him to do—share the gospel with pagans. And God honored it with souls harvested for the kingdom.

"How dare they criticize me! Do they not know who I am?"

No, not Peter. No place for cockiness here. Instead he defused the situation with a proven tactic: "Peter began and explained everything to them precisely as it had happened" (Acts 11:4).

Details. "Precisely," the Scriptures say. The word from the original could be translated "in an orderly sequence." With a full thirteen verses in Acts (and really probably a lot more words than are given in Luke's condensed version) Peter gave a clear play by play of the events that bothered his friends.[3] No stone was left unturned that might help his friends understand all that had taken place.

And the payoff? "When they heard this, they had no further objections and praised God, saying, 'So then, God has granted even the Gentiles repentance unto life'" (Acts 11:18).

That's not always going to work. But assuming you have a critic who is willing to hear, a careful explanation of the events can change the way the story is read. Maybe he didn't have all the facts. Maybe you shared information that was inadvertently inferior. Maybe it allowed for other conclusions. Now is the time for details, a no-holds-barred case history. Give the data, all the data, and nothing but the data.

Think back over what you are now criticized for—is there anything else that your critic needs to know? Not your subjective feelings, but objective facts that are verifiable by both you and the other person? What you may consider insignificant may be the missing strand to the riddle. If the person is trying to put it all together—whether it is her place to do so or not—she can't get an accurate read without all the text. Only God is under absolutely no obligation to make explanations. For the rest of us, it's a fact of life—especially the chapters marked "maintaining relationships."

A leader in a church I once pastored turned auditor. His primary account was me. Every move I made was an entry on his mental ledger. If you have been there, you know the feeling. It's no fun to be "audited," whether by a spouse, parent, neighbor, worker, or church member. I was taken back, because I thought our relationship was sound. Then I found out the reason for the balance sheet. "Pastor, you don't seem to care about some of our sheep." That cut deeply.

I asked for specifics, and he countered with the name of an individual who had left the church in a miff. Out of my file I pulled a letter received from this upset member. In it was a reference to a previous three-hour meeting at a coffee shop. When I read that portion of the letter, he replied, "You mean you met with him for three hours one afternoon? Pastor, forgive me. I shouldn't have been so quick to believe what I heard." A friendship on the rocks was saved and today is stronger than ever.

Second-hand information is often all our critics work from. They should know better, but it's still done. Tell them the rest of the story. Tell them all the "why" behind what you have done.

A husband and wife were celebrating fifty years of marriage. After spending most of the day with relatives and friends at a large celebration given in their honor, the two made it back home. Before retiring, they decided to have a little snack of tea with bread and butter. In the kitchen, the husband opened up a new loaf of bread and handed the end piece to his wife. She exploded. "For fifty years with every new loaf of bread you've dumped the heel on me! It's thoughtless! It's rude! And I am just not going to take it anymore!" The husband, stunned, softly said: "But it's my favorite piece."[4]

Tell them the rest of the story. Tell them all the "why" behind what you have done.

AFFIRMATION

An old American proverb runs: "Flattery is soft soap, and soap is 90 percent *lye*." For sure, you don't want to flatter in that negative sense, but genuine praise offered to your critic is not doing that. A truthful, sincere compliment is anything but soft soap.

Sometimes we cannot do anything about the bone being picked. But if we sit back and just let things go, we can expect a main-engine launch, with the person blowing sky-high. All it takes from us is a push of the button: a careless word, no words, a glare, a back turned. To download some of the tension, try genuine honor. Benjamin Disraeli said, "I have observed that nothing ever perplexes an adversary so much as an appeal to his honor."[5]

Heartfelt applause calculated to lower his critics' blood pressure was a tactic used successfully by one of the great generals of Israel's history:

> Now the Ephraimites asked Gideon, "Why have you treated us like this? Why didn't you call us when you went to fight Midian?" And they criticized him sharply. But he answered them, "What have I accomplished compared to you? Aren't the gleanings of Ephraim's grapes better than the full grape harvest of Abiezer? God gave Oreb and Zeeb, the Midianite leaders, into your hands. What was I able to do compared to you?" At this, their resentment against him subsided.
>
> —JUDGES 8:1-3

Someone has said, "I had rather that true and faithful teachers should rebuke and condemn me, and reprove my ways, than that hypocrites should flatter me and applaud me as a saint." Gideon was true and faithful. He was not into two-faced flattery. But given the situation he faced—a potential split of the young Jewish nation over who had the greatest military victory—this was not the time to rebuke and condemn. Sure there was probably some jealousy. Yes, maybe the critics were immature. But Gideon knew that a benign reply was in order. "A gentle answer turns away wrath, but a harsh word stirs up anger" (Prov. 15:1). And the gentle answer he chose was filled with hearty kudos. It was not just polite applause, something you do because you know you are supposed to. The Ephraimites, having accomplished something significant, deserved praise.

Is the one you are called to serve breathing down your neck? Could it be that, like the Ephraimites, he or she feels overshadowed by some of what you have done? Then compliment your critic on tasks well-done. Offer congratulations. Express your admiration. See the person as more consequential than yourself. "Do nothing out of selfish ambition or vain conceit, but in humility consider others better than yourselves" (Phil. 2:3).

When is it inappropriate to praise a critical person? One: When you are being criticized for outright sin, and the criticism is accurate. If what is said is true, the tension you feel will be relieved in only one way: confession. Two: When you are *falsely* accused of sin. Sin is a serious charge, obviously more serious than those "against you" realize or they would have done their homework.

But much criticism is like that of the tribe of Ephraim, a complaint over judgment calls. Is it possible to maintain integrity and loosen tension through a kind word of commendation? If so, don't hesitate to do it in a tasteful and timely manner. And continue to do it. A benchmark for sincerity is consistency. It verifies that when you took the heat, you spoke with veracity.

Harry S. Truman said, "If somebody throws a brick at me, I can catch it and throw it back. But when somebody awards a decoration to me, I am out of words."[6] An almost unbeatable way to neutralize critics is to make them your friends. Even if it scares them, try praising those who have made ministry hard for you.

THE EYES HAVE IT

Suppose the complaint against you is covered with absolutely no facts at all. It stands buck naked of any truth. You did not say what you are said to have said. You did not do what you are said to have done. This time you are very certain that your words and actions are guiltless in the sight of the Lord. Your critic, though, obviously thinks otherwise. He sees what you did as wrong. He hears what you said as wrong. Then what can be done to defuse the situation?

Maybe nothing.

If your behavior has been right in the sight of the Lord, and your critic doesn't buy it, you may sit at an impasse. But sometimes being right in the sight of the Lord is not enough.

"Blaine," you ask, "what kind of remark is that? If you do what is right in His eyes, what other eyes really matter?"

People's.

Listen to Paul as he talks money: "We want to avoid any criticism of the way we administer this liberal gift. For we are taking pains to do what is right, not only in the eyes of the Lord but also in the eyes of men" (2 Cor. 8:20–21).

The apostle was concerned that the financial gift, which he was to pick up at Corinth and deliver to Jerusalem, would be properly handled, not only according to God's audit but according to man's audits, too. The Lord wasn't going to see any funny stuff done with the books; nothing would raise suspicions in the saints either.

Did this mean that Paul was serving two masters? If push came to shove, did he try to please both God and men?

Of course not. The apostle recognized that it is possible to do what's right in the eyes of the Lord, who sees the puzzle all put together, and appear to do what is wrong in the eyes of men, who see only scattered pieces. You don't have to worry that God may get the wrong idea; omniscience takes care of that. Though our critics sometimes act all-knowing, their knowledge is anything but perfect. Try scant, sparse, unsophisticated, paltry, narrow, provincial, often lacking in the details that are necessary for making wise decisions.

For sure there is a difference between "being seen as doing what's right" and "making a show of doing what's right." The latter betrayed the Pharisees' logo: "Look at me." What the apostle urged was covering bases—doing everything possible to foil Satan from secreting thoughts into the mind of a dormant critic:

- "I wonder what he is doing with that money."
- "His doors are closed, and they are together alone. You don't suppose they are . . . ?"

In fallen minds, thoughts like these appear with ease even when there is no hint of impropriety. They rush in when something we do looks a little questionable.

This is a compelling principle when it comes to criticism: *Grievances are often incurred because we do what is honorable in the sight of God with absolute disregard for what is honorable in the sight of men.* We know it is right. God knows it is right. But our critic does not. To him it appears otherwise.

Learn to safeguard yourself like Paul. Stop and ask yourself:

- What did it look like to her?
- What did it sound like to him?
- Is it possible, given the tone of society, that wrong was thought of me because others have done wrong in a similar situation?
- Was her perspective such that she could not really see all that I was doing?
- What would I think if, knowing only what he knew, I saw him doing the very same thing?

You can never be too careful. Use sanctified common sense for the sake of the Lord and those God has called you to serve:

- Don't have lunch alone with someone of the opposite sex, unless it is the one you are married to.
- Let your mate know where you are at all times. How they can reach you. When you will be back. Stay accountable to them. Don't allow others to raise suspicions in their minds.
- Avoid closed doors with a person of the opposite gender, if it is not your spouse. Stay in the public's eye. If you must meet with them, do it in the presence of a third party. That includes counseling situations. No exceptions. Period. If it is your supervisor who wants the door closed, tell your supervisor you don't want the door closed. If he does not agree, then trust God, and tell him to find another employee.
- Don't handle other people's money, especially money they are giving to the church. "Pastor, I forgot to put this in the plate. Would you see that it gets in?" I won't. I direct them to someone else or tell them to give it next Sunday.

- Keep records like a legalist. Your use of your ministry resources. Your use of your ministry time. Don't waste what others have entrusted to you.
- And be on time for office hours and all appointments.

"But, Blaine, my people trust me. It's only a few who are making noise."

That's great, but you want to solidify trust, not presume upon it. Your goal is to do both what's right in the sight of omniscient God and in the sight of the non-omniscient people you serve. If you live intentionally with that goal, it's likely fewer people will turn analytical of you.

If it's too late for that ounce of prevention, and the bomb is ticking, talk to your critic from his vista. Tell him that you have just realized there is validity to his criticism, given his perspective. You can really understand why he has thought what he has thought. Then proceed to document as well as possible the "why" of the discrepancy. And from now on, take into account all eyes.

ADVERSARY TO ADVOCATE

The frog informed the princess: "You may not believe this, but I was a good-looking prince until a wicked hag put a spell on me. One kiss from you and . . . poof . . . I'm that handsome prince again. Then we can wed, move into the villa with my mom, and you can cook me gourmet dinners, fix me bedtime snacks, wash my clothes, bear my children, and feel happy for doing so forever."

That night, the princess had frog's legs for dinner.

Have you ever wanted to do that—"fry" the one who has made life tough for you? Of course, if you do it you will lose a relationship, maybe forever.

Look at how the apostles graciously handled their critics in Acts 6:

In those days when the number of disciples was increasing, the Grecian Jews among them complained against the Hebraic Jews because their widows were being overlooked in the daily distribution of food. So the Twelve gathered all the disciples together and said, "It would not be right for us to neglect the ministry of the word of God in order to wait on tables. Brothers, choose seven men from among you who are known to be full of the Spirit and wisdom. We will turn this responsibility over to them and will give our attention to prayer and the ministry of the word."

This proposal pleased the whole group. They chose Stephen, a man full of faith and of the Holy Spirit; also Philip, Procorus, Nicanor, Timon, Parmenas, and Nicolas from Antioch, a convert to Judaism. They presented these men to the apostles, who prayed and laid their hands on them.

So the word of God spread. The number of disciples in Jerusalem increased rapidly, and a large number of priests became obedient to the faith.

–VV. 1–7

Because the apostles refused to have frog's legs for supper, the early church was saved from a tear that might have ripped at the fabric of faith for centuries.

There was a problem. The criticism rattled with truth: Grecian widows *were* being overlooked. It was unintentional, without latent prejudices. But to maintain priorities and do all that needed to be done, the apostles simply were strapped for time. But there still was a problem, one that reflected upon their leadership. People under their care were slipping through the cracks.

- "You should have done it."
- "No, we should not have; that's your concern."

There was no dodging the matter, no blame smeared. The apostles humbly agreed that a solution was necessary, and the Twelve turned to their critics—the very persons making life tumultuous for them—to find it.

Certainly the apostolic leadership itself could have selected spiritual men "full of the Spirit and wisdom" just as good as, if not better than, their riled flock. But prudence dictated otherwise. Those criticized were wise enough to incorporate their critics into the process to find a solution. Result? "This proposal pleased the whole group."

The apostles' technique assumes that we acknowledge the problem, even though it runs against our pride. It may not be our fault. Perhaps, even as the apostles, we did not realize a problem existed until the matter went public. But there will never be relief from tension if we, the criticized, balk, circumvent the difficulty, and stymie the discussion. That is not how secure children of God operate. Instead, exhibit maturity:

- "Yes, I think I am hearing what you are saying. What do you suggest?"
- "I didn't realize that before. Would you be willing to help me out in seeing this matter is handled correctly?"
- "I didn't know that. Let's do this. . . . What do you think about it?"
- "You've got me thinking now. Can we sit down and brainstorm ways we might be able to solve this problem?"

Such invitations to take part build commitment for teamwork. It's not just *you* that will solve the problem. You make a commitment to work with your critic to solve the problem *together,* even though you are the one getting nailed.

When we take this approach, we communicate several things to the one making things tough for us:

- I respect you, even though you just picked me apart.
- I have not arrived.
- I value your input.
- I want to work together with you, not in competition against you.
- I believe there is a solution to this problem and I need you to help find it.

Make an honest effort to become a "team" with your critic. Resist the urge to have frog legs for supper.

YES?

In some ways, ministry is like marriage. You pour yourself into it, your very life. It's where you live. It's where you work. It's where you worship. And because ministry is intensely relationship oriented, it's where you can get hurt, and hurt bad . . . gutted by careless words.

tick . . .

tick . . .

tick . . .

Yes?

Then defuse it. Don't ignore relational problems. To ignore them is to risk losing it all. Take your role seriously as a peacemaker; otherwise, the tension can accelerate to crisis speed.

Give your critic what God gave to His critics—a way to reestablish a relationship. With God, it was done through the death of His Son. "For God so loved the world that he gave his one and only Son, that whoever believes in him shall not perish but have eternal life" (John 3:16). He did everything possible to see that we could forever have a relationship with Him as His child. All that we had to do was receive it—"whoever believes in him." If there is no relationship between Him and us, it is because of us, not Him.

Do as God. Do everything possible to ensure that the relationship between you and your critic flourishes. No, it is not easy. Yes, you and you alone must take the initiative if it is to happen. Do everything possible so that if there is no relationship, it's not because of you.

This is not a future decision. This is a "now" decision that may very well have an impact on what will happen in the future between you and those who are not your fans. It could determine where there can ever again be a relationship that blesses. It could determine if there will ever be a relationship at all.

To put off taking the initiative until you feel like it or until a better time is to place your ministry deeper in the ditch. You cannot afford to just sit back and hope things get better. Reality warns that they will not. Something must change, and that something includes you. Do everything possible to salvage what was once dear to you. *Everything possible* embraces details, genuine praise, rightness in all eyes, and teamwork. With all your might, make it happen.

    tick . . .

    tick . . .

    tick . . .

By God's grace, save your ministry to those you are called to serve.

Chapter 10

WHEN YOU DON'T
WANT TO FORGIVE

Ramath Lehi. Remember it? Probably not. You won't find it on the Travel Channel or in El Al's vacation getaways. But in Samson's day it was a top-ten tourist attraction. If you couldn't see the other nine, you made sure you saw Ramath Lehi.

> Finding a fresh jawbone of a donkey, he grabbed it and struck down a thousand men.
> Then Samson said,
>
> "With a donkey's jawbone
> I have made donkeys of them.
>
> With a donkey's jawbone
> I have killed a thousand men."
> When he finished speaking, he threw away the jawbone; and the place was called Ramath Lehi.
> –JUDGES 15:15–17

By busloads they came. With the final score, Samson 1000, Philistines 0, people just had to walk the battleground and see the venue where that bloody weapon was slung. And from then on the locals called that tract of land "Jawbone Hill." That's what Ramath Lehi means. This was the place where one jawbone bludgeoned so many. Jawbones still bludgeon. A killer then. A killer now.

- "You could have learned a lot from your predecessor. He knew how to do it."
- "Ineffective. There's just no other way to say it. You are simply ineffective."
- "My child wouldn't do that."
- "We don't get anything out of what you say."
- "If God really had His hand on you, don't you think our attendance would at least equal what they are running on the other side of town?"
- "We've met frequently, prayed about it a lot, and are convinced it's time for new leadership."

They were killers then; they are killers now. Jawbones destroy people. Back then it was the jawbone of a donkey. Today it is the jawbones of . . . youth, the parents of youth, congregations, elders, deacons, pastors, staff members, fellow missionaries, young, old, middle-aged, Christian, non-Christian. It's the jawbones of those who, with their words, beat their neighbor to an emotional death.

And the carnage is you. Clubbed. Lacerated. Bleeding. You die by giving up on others, yourself, the Lord; die by anger that razes everything in sight, including you.

But life goes on. With or without you, it goes on.

With you? It's because you chose to make the necessary adjustments visited in this book. And because you do, the wounds heal; possibly with some scarring, but not enough to leave you unrecognizable. And in doing so, you delight in your loved ones, especially your family. You make new memories. You smile. You laugh. You savor old friends. You make new friends. Treasure God's gifts. Cherish the Lord. You minister! You believe what Paul said to Timothy, that God "richly provides us with everything for our enjoyment" (1 Tim. 6:17c). You believe it and enjoy it all, especially Him.

Without you? Friends will still be out there. Family members will be around. There will be new people to meet. New opportunities to jump on. And certainly, the Lord will never leave or forsake you. But life goes on without you. The children get older. Parents age. Loved ones pass away. Friends face new challenges and crises. Ministry needs are greater than ever. But you miss it all. There's little merging. The focus has changed. Something has consumed you—your critic.

THE WEED SEED

It's been said that come Valentine's Day, you probably won't find the following messages in your local card shop:

- "Looking back over the years that we've been together, I can't help but wonder: What was I thinking?"
- "As the days go by, I think of how lucky I am . . . that you're not here to ruin it for me."
- "Before you go, take this knife out of my back. You'll probably need it again."
- "I'm so miserable without you. . . . It's almost like you're here."

Animosity. Disgust. Scorn. Disdain. Venom. Vindictiveness. Bitterness—or as the writer to the Hebrews put it, a "bitter root" (12:15).

Is it always such a malicious root? No, viciousness is seldom the first calling card of bitterness. It starts seedlike. Maybe with a phone call, an appointment, a passing conversation or, more likely, out on the grapevine. Someone to whom we've given time, energy, and gifts hurts us. What's said is untrue. How it's said is uncalled for. And the fallout is significant.

We mull it over. We speculate. We weigh. In the quiet confines of the heart, we work the soil. Water. Fertilize. Like a gardener, we hoe, sprinkle, and hoe some more, making sure the seed has all it needs to do what seeds are known to do.

Success! Stringy threadlike fibers from the seed twine their way through the dirt. They branch out with no rhyme or reason . . . except for one thready fiber. It's different. It has both purpose and resolve. It's the taproot.

Deep into the soil of the heart the taproot sinks and grows ever so

fast. In fact, by the time the stem breaks ground—questionable attitudes, acid-laced words, icy silence, avoidance—the root has grown so
large it reshapes the heart. Its strands intermingle with spiritual tissue. Oh, does it ever hurt to tug on it!

If this sprout remained sequestered, then one might pity only its
owner, the bitter person whose company few enjoy. But the shoot is
not quarantined. The foliage desecrates homes and churches, doing
more damage to the cause of Christ than sexual licentiousness ever
did. Bitterness is deadly poison.

No wonder the warning: "See to it that no one misses the grace of
God and that no bitter root grows up to cause trouble and defile many"
(Heb. 12:15). Paul tells us, "Get rid of all bitterness, rage and anger,
brawling and slander, along with every form of malice" (Eph. 4:31).

Maybe you are staring at a crossroads. As you've read this book,
outward circumstances probably haven't changed. And if they have
changed the change may be for the worse. But life goes on. Will it go
on with you?

After all you've been through, can you still make what's left of your
ministry house into a home? Will you continue to do those extras
that make it what only you can? Will you nurture those whom God
has called you to serve? Will you "be there" spiritually and emotionally when people need you the most? Will you "be there" when your
family needs you the most? Are you "there" now?

Will you continue to model spiritual excellence in your choices for
those who look up to you? Will you do the same with your diligence
behind the scenes as you prepare to publicly serve? Will you love the
Lord God where you are with all your heart, soul, mind, and strength?
Will you lead from love? Life goes on. Will it go on with you? Dear
servant: Is it not time to toss what's been used on you over on Jawbone Hill?

REPRIEVE

There's a life God wants you to live. He does have a future for you.
Whether you are still unjustly criticized or now struggle only with its
fallout, this matter must be put to rest. To enjoy your Lord and all
that He has for you, there must be closure.

- "I will go on."
- "For Him, I will be productive."
- "As an expression of my gratitude, I will savor His gifts to me."

To do so assumes we've picked the jawbone up. We really do want to get rid of it. Cocked for the toss, at just the right moment, the arm gets that mental command: "Release it. Let it go. Don't hold on to it any longer."

If you do hold on to it, you may hurt your arm. Maybe even get clobbered. You've got to free it, to send it on its way. You must open the grasp of your fist and liberate that jawbone. "Bear with each other and forgive whatever grievances you may have against one another. Forgive as the Lord forgave you" (Col. 3:13).

Forgiveness. More than anything else, that will send both you and the jawbone on your merry ways. For you, it will mean pressing on in all that your Lord has for you. For that jawbone, no longer are you at its mercy.

- What was said is forgiven.
- The way it was said is forgiven.
- The carelessness in saying it is forgiven.
- The refusal to hear the truth is forgiven.
- The hurt that it caused is forgiven.
- The aftermath that it yielded is forgiven.

No longer do you hold on to the jawbone. You let it go. You send it on its way. That is what the word *forgiveness* means. In sending it on its way, you cancel the debt incurred by your critics through their involvement in all of the above.

To forgive does not mean you no longer can say what needs to be said. Biblical admonishments are not negated: "So watch yourselves. If your brother sins, rebuke him, and if he repents, forgive him" (Luke 17:3). And for sure, to forgive does not mean you go public: "I want you to know something: I've forgiven you." Your critic doesn't see the need for your forgiveness. Besides, to say unsolicited "I've forgiven you" oozes with pride. That smells to high heaven.

No, forgiveness is granted, whether or not it's received. Should your critic ever come to realize that he has committed a spiritual crime—with his words attempted to destroy a member of the body of Christ—then you are prepared to outwardly express what you inwardly have already done. "So watch yourselves. If your brother sins, rebuke him, and if he repents, forgive him. If he sins against you seven times in a day, and seven times comes back to you and says, 'I repent,' forgive him" (Luke 17:3–4).

It's easy to talk about forgiveness—teach on it; preach on it; counsel others to do it. It's easy to do three points and a poem on forgiveness when you have not been hurt. That's hitting a plastic ball off of a tee with an oversized plastic bat. That's T-ball stuff.

But when the word-blast guts, and the soul gets the wind knocked out of it, sermonizing is not going to do it. You are not just talking about a problem. You are not just telling others about your problem. You are saying the past is the past. It's over. There's nothing that can be done to undo what was done. You are now choosing to change the future. You now choose to forgive.

Forgiveness is the road to take. There's mountain fresh air for the soul. The scenic vistas are breathtaking. This road is the safest route home. It is the only way to survive the devastation from unscrupulous criticism. It's what will thump yet another jawbone on the dirt over on Jawbone Hill.

The following are suggested pitching tips.

TIP: *Return to the Scene*

A new business opened, and flowers were sent for the occasion. When the owner read "Rest in Peace" on the card he was livid and let the florist know in no uncertain terms he was livid over such a stupid blunder. The florist said, "Sir, I'm really sorry for the mistake, but if you think you are angry, just imagine that somewhere there is a funeral taking place today with a card that reads, 'Congratulations on your new location.'"

Location, location, location. Maybe for you where it happened was a new location—a new ministry, a new place to eat, a new conference room. Maybe it was an old familiar place—an office, an auditorium, a boardroom. Whichever. *Somewhere* you were verbally undressed. It is now the scene of the crime and bears a stigma.

You know where you should meet with the Lord next? Right there. Get as close to that location as you can and encounter the Lord in worship. Assuming you were wronged, it was there that you were sinned against. It's where you ought to be when you release your grip. Spiritual transactions don't have to have that sort of symbolism, but it can help. We are to worship our Lord in spirit and truth. But symbols can seal to our hearts the transactions we make. There is a physical side to being spiritual. As baptism and communion outwardly prompt us to reflect over an inward reality, the place where you were piled on can likewise stir feeling. "Because of what took place in this room, I'm suffering today. In this building I was shamed." With those feelings, bowing before the Lord is anything but a theological exercise.

"Lord, I was injured on this very spot. Being in this place now, there is a surge of both pain and resentment. . . . Lord, I come back here to say to you . . . 'I forgive them.'"

Precedent? There is really little, except maybe at the cross. Those who screamed for His blood, pounded the nails, and thumbed their noses at God—the Lord forgave them right where it took place.

> When they came to the place called the Skull, there they crucified him, along with the criminals—one on his right, the other on his left. Jesus said, "Father, forgive them, for they do not know what they are doing."
>
> —LUKE 23:33–34A

Do the same. You will not struggle with any stronger feelings of anger than when you quietly return to the scene of the offense. There forgive. As far as you are concerned, clear your critic of all charges. Pardon him. From your heart of hearts grant a reprieve. Before the Lord, absolve him. Leave that place having torn up every debt your accuser has incurred in his treatment of you.

What was said. The way it was said. The consequences.

Shred each of them. You will walk away a different person.

A drill sergeant who had just chewed out a new recruit ended his rant by saying, "I guess when I die you'll come and dance on my grave." The kid said, "Not me, Sarge. I promised myself that when I got out of the Army, I'd never stand in another line."

Friend, others may want to dance. It's conceivable that over the years your critic has hurt more than you. Let them dance. But not you. Don't entertain the thought of even a waltz. You be different. If possible, go back to where it happened and forgive. Then worship.

TIP: *Picture them mentally*

When God forgives, God sees. The guilty party is forever before His eyes. Omniscience makes that so. When the Savior chooses to rub out the moral charge made against the sinner, it is not done in some heavenly accounting office in a wing off the throne room: "Open the books, erase the debt, rebalance the spread sheet—Next. . . ."

God sees the guilty party—face, physique, spirit, and soul. All of the person is before Him. Forgiveness is not just an electronic transfer of spiritual funds.

Suggestion number two? Mentally place your critic before you on the couch or in the chair or possibly over across the table. Presume he is right there. Whether or not you are able to go back to the location where you were criticized, set your accuser down in front of you (gently), and forgive.

We are not talking Eastern meditation techniques. Imaging has no place in New Testament theology. We *are* talking about remembering the person who has hurt us for the sake of this matter of forgiveness. We cannot afford to see it as some hygienic legal transaction. Bowing down before the Lord with the memories of our critic before us will go far in sealing this ministry to our hearts. There is only one step better, and that is to do it, unknown to your critic, in his actual presence.

Two leaders in a church I once pastored withdrew from my fan club. (In the Greek, that means, when it came to me, they felt an unusual freedom to speak their minds.) One of the most liberating things I ever did happened without any planning on my part. The two served as greeters one Sunday morning. As I sat on the platform watching them lead guests in, I started talking to the Lord in my heart: "Father, you know what Charles said. You know what he continues to say and the devastating fallout it's already had. Lord, looking at him right now, I want to revoke any right I think I have to hold against him what he has done. And Rob, too. His talk has done much harm. It has so pained my family. Lord, in Your presence in full view of him, I forgive."

When I met those two following the morning service, I felt like a new pastor. For the first time in months, I really meant it when I said, "Good to see you!"

If you sit on a platform and can look at your critics unobserved, that is an opportunity to do the same. Before a meeting begins as your critics file in is another chance, or as you see them while you mill around with others at a "get together." You probably will see them again. Talk to the Lord in full view. It was in full view of His critics that our Lord said, "Father, forgive them, for they do not know what they are doing" (Luke 23:34a). Anything that will move us to genuinely forgive another is worth an honest try. The stakes are too high. Not to forgive is to slam the prison door . . . on yourself.

TIP: *Write It Down*

A study reveals that more than half of Americans lose their TV remote between one and five times a week, while 11 percent misplace it six to ten times. Sixty-three percent of those who've lost their remotes spend five minutes searching for them, and 16 percent spend ten minutes. Most often the device is hiding in or under the furniture or in a nearby room, but 6 percent say they usually find it in the fridge.[1]

When a person hurts us, we know when it happened, where it happened, and why it happened. We also know how to find at once all the feelings that went with it. It is one of those unstated laws of the Medes, and the Persians, and the humans: Even though we've genuinely forgiven, if someone has hurt us, it's going to come up again. It may be months, weeks, days, or hours later, but it will come up again. We will find ourselves trying to piece back together that shredded document that canceled all our critic's debts.

But not so with our Lord:

> As far as the east is from the west,
> so far has he removed our transgressions from us.
>
> —PSALM 103:12

In your love you kept me
from the pit of destruction;

you have put all my sins
behind your back.

—ISAIAH 38:17B

I, even I, am he who blots out
your transgressions, for my own sake,
and remembers your sins no more.

—ISAIAH 43:25

When the Lord forgives our sin, it is never *un*forgiven. For Him forgiveness is irrevocable. It is final. Decisive. Definitive. The end. What He does from His heart, based on the shed blood of the Lord Jesus, is done for good. No second thoughts. No memory lapses.

Not so with us; that makes having a record of your forgiveness in black and white a valuable reminder. Pull out the notebook. Leaf through the pages. There it is, a date and time when you forgave your critic.

With that graphic reminder in front of you, a decision must be made. Either you were kidding yourself back then—unlikely if you made the effort to write it down—or you are renouncing your previous action. Either way, you force yourself afresh to observe God's priority: "Forgive whatever grievances you may have against one another" (Col. 3:13b).

Whether we return to where we were criticized, envision the person before us, write down the forgiveness, or a combination of the three, these are ways to drive a stake deep into our spiritual ground—a stake that we can return to in the days that lie ahead. Should we choose to pick up that jawbone again, there's a built-in leash for the Spirit of God to use: "But I forgave him. I vividly remember bowing before the Lord and forgiving my brother."

C. S. Lewis said, "We all agree that forgiveness is a beautiful idea until we have to practice it."[2]

Practice it.

TIP: *Actions Speak*

One seasoned individual prayed: "Grant me the senility to forget the people I never liked anyway, the good fortune to run into the ones I do, and the eyesight to tell the difference."[3]

So much for loving your neighbor as yourself. Yet Jesus said, "'Love the Lord your God with all your heart and with all your soul and with all your mind.' This is the first and greatest commandment. And the second is like it: 'Love your neighbor as yourself'" (Matt. 22:37–39).

Paul declared, "The commandments, 'Do not commit adultery,' 'Do not murder,' 'Do not steal,' 'Do not covet,' and whatever other commandment there may be, are summed up in this one rule: 'Love your neighbor as yourself'" (Rom. 13:9). He wrote the Galatians, "The entire law is summed up in a single command: 'Love your neighbor as yourself'" (Gal. 5:14).

James reminds us, "If you really keep the royal law found in Scripture, 'Love your neighbor as yourself,' you are doing right" (James 2:8).

And where in the Old Testament did that "second" commandment, "the royal law," come from? It's found in a cluster of "do nots."

Do not go about spreading slander among your people. Do not do anything that endangers your neighbor's life. I am the LORD.

Do not hate your brother in your heart. Rebuke your neighbor frankly so you will not share in his guilt.

Do not seek revenge or bear a grudge against one of your people, but love your neighbor as yourself. I am the LORD.

–LEVITICUS 19:16–18

The New Testament works out the positive side of the "do nots." It's insufficient to *not* spread dirt, to *not* endanger your neighbor, to *not* hate, to *not* seek revenge or bear a grudge. If that is the extent of your behavior toward your critic—an itemized catalog of things that you have not done—it's incomplete.

The Lord expects the flip side: "But love your neighbor as yourself. I am the LORD"(Lev. 19:18b). That sums it all up. Along with a ledger of things it has not done, love includes a list of things it has done—things that God would call good.

Remember Malchus? Maybe this will help: "Then Simon Peter, who had a sword, drew it and struck the high priest's servant, cutting off his right ear. (The servant's name was Malchus.)" (John 18:10). Clear-cut, decisive, and "good-bye head," except for Simon Peter's less than stellar performance. A soldier he was not. Gratefully for Malchus, the "act first, think later" fisherman was slightly off target.

Our Lord's response? In the garden as He was being betrayed, "Jesus commanded Peter, 'Put your sword away!'" (John 18:11a). "No more of this!" (Luke 22:51a). Though Malchus was in the hunt for Jesus that night with Judas and his posse, no retaliation. No "Go for it, Peter—you can do it!" No slander. No hatred. No bearing a grudge. Our Lord's response embraced all of the "do nots." But His love included so much more—resourcefulness, ingenuity, creativity, the good. "And he touched the man's ear and healed him" (v. 51b).

Do you love like that? Are you resourceful? Do you show imagination? Would heaven call it "good"? Do you really love your critic as yourself?

That's what authentic forgiveness does. Because your critic is your neighbor, you can't run him down. You can't bloody up his future by flailing away with an emotional sword. But more than that: you can't sit back and relax. You must actively do good for him. Forgiveness that loves asserts itself to touch the person's life.

It takes him out for coffee. It expresses genuine concern for his concerns. It comes to his defense when others falsely accuse. It always, always, always gives him the benefit of the doubt. It expresses appreciation for the good that he does. It prays and prays and prays.

You do for your critic what you would really appreciate him doing for you. If it would be a blessing to yourself, you do it for the one who has been anything but a blessing to you. If you wouldn't like it done to you, you won't do it to him. You love your critic as yourself.

Doing good—not because it is the spiritual thing to do but because you love with a love that springs from Christ living within. When you begin to experience that kind of love as an act of your regenerated will, it won't be long before you hear a "thump" over there on Jawbone Hill.

YOU'VE JUST GOT TO

So much for tips. The point is you've got to forgive. You cannot consider yourself a serious follower of Jesus Christ and not forgive. Listen to what Jesus said:

> And when you stand praying, if you hold anything against anyone, forgive him, so that your Father in heaven may forgive you your sins.
>
> —MARK 11:25

> Forgive, and you will be forgiven.
>
> —LUKE 6:37C

In telling us how to talk to God, Jesus taught us to pray in the Lord's Prayer: "Forgive us our debts, as we also have forgiven our debtors" (Matt. 6:12). Do you remember the lone footnote He attached to that model prayer? "For if you forgive men when they sin against you, your heavenly Father will also forgive you. But if you do not forgive men their sins, your Father will not forgive your sins" (vv. 14–15).

Peter picked up enough to know that forgiveness was serious business and so asked Jesus, "'Lord, how often shall my brother sin against me and I forgive him? Up to seven times?' Jesus said to him, 'I do not say to you, up to seven times, but up to seventy times seven'" (Matt. 18:21–22 NASB).

Translation? "If you are still counting, you are not forgiving." And to make sure it stuck, the Lord nailed this truth down with a story:

> "Therefore, the kingdom of heaven is like a king who wanted to settle accounts with his servants. As he began the settlement, a man who owed him ten thousand talents was brought to him. Since he was not able to pay, the master ordered that he and his wife and his children and all that he had be sold to repay the debt.
>
> "The servant fell on his knees before him. 'Be patient with me,' he begged, 'and I will pay back everything.' The servant's master took pity on him, canceled the debt and let him go.

"But when that servant went out, he found one of his fellow servants who owed him a hundred denarii. He grabbed him and began to choke him. 'Pay back what you owe me!' he demanded.

"His fellow servant fell to his knees and begged him, 'Be patient with me, and I will pay you back.'

"But he refused. Instead, he went off and had the man thrown into prison until he could pay the debt. When the other servants saw what had happened, they were greatly distressed and went and told their master everything that had happened.

"Then the master called the servant in. 'You wicked servant,' he said, 'I canceled all that debt of yours because you begged me to. Shouldn't you have had mercy on your fellow servant just as I had on you?' In anger his master turned him over to the jailers to be tortured, until he should pay back all he owed.

"This is how my heavenly Father will treat each of you unless you forgive your brother from your heart."

—MATTHEW 18:23–35

Friend, grab your thoughts by the seat of the britches and make them correspond to the way things really are! You've got to take your will and force it to fit what's real. You are to forgive. That's reality. To create your own world and think you can coddle whatever was done to you by another and be just fine is to flirt with disaster. That's a reality makeover. It simply does not match what Jesus Christ reveals. Truth is contingent on Him, not you. The need to forgive is so whether you stand with it or not, and if you are smart, you will vigorously embrace it. Fellow servant, your soul is more important than any hurt.

And what about the insults, the sneers, the vehemence, the shredded flesh and blood—all best described as savage? Can you honestly visualize the cross and just let your need to forgive ride? When an eternal cauldron of boiling evil was poured over the very Son of God, can you really live with yourself and not do what the Lord says to do? Was it not your evil that caused divine wrath to turn Jesus' soul into a burning hell? Was it not your lying, your deceit, your anger, your whatever you have done that no one else knows that you have done, that turned Jesus' heart into an eternal inferno? Friend, when Jesus Christ cried, "My God, my God, why have you forsaken me?" (Matt. 27:36b), the answer is you. It's me. "God made him who had no sin to be sin for us, so that in him we might become the righteousness of God" (2 Cor. 5:21). If you have yet to forgive your critic, you need to repent.

Any thorns on your brow?

Did blood blur your vision?

Were you spit on? In your hair? In your eyes?

Were your clothes clawed off you?

Were you whipped?

Were you repeatedly whipped?

Did a mob scream for your flesh?

Any nails rip open your palms?

Any slits in your feet?

Did you heave?

Did you continue to heave?

Did you endure it alone?

Did you become all the filth the world has known? All that it will ever know?

Was it your first time to ever come in contact with moral waste?

Was the stench such that the Father had to turn His back on you?

Upon you, did He pour out His wrath? Did His holy anger surge, breaker after breaker smashing in on your body, soul, and spirit?

Honestly, did you experience anybody's forever hell, including your own, all compressed into six hours?

In comparison, so little has been done to you. The consequences so meager. The pain so marginal. To refuse to forgive your critic is to be unmoved by the heart of God. Unbelievable. Simply unbelievable. Jesus Christ went through too much for you to hang on to that jawbone. Release it. Give it a toss. Chuck what's been used on you over on Jawbone Hill. "Bear with each other and forgive whatever grievances you may have against one another. Forgive as the Lord forgave you" (Col. 3:13). Friend, let it go.

May the Lord give you discernment to realize what's really at stake with the hurt you've endured. And may you use the wisdom and grace that comes from above to do what needs to be done.

Who knows? This could be the new beginning you've so longed for.

As far as God is concerned, it is.

ENDNOTES

Introduction: A Terrorist?

1. Edythe Draper, *Draper's Book of Quotations for the Christian World* (Wheaton, Ill.: Tyndale House, 1992), 2050.
2. "Letter to Mr. Hume, Washington Post Music Critic," as recorded by the National Archives and Records Administration, Truman Library.
3. William Willimon, "You Need a Good Priest," *Preaching Today*, audio sermons, tape no. 106.

Chapter 1: When You Can't Take Any More

1. Edythe Draper, *Draper's Book of Quotations for the Christian World* (Wheaton, Ill.: Tyndale House, 1992), 9631.
2. Cal and Rose Samra, *Holy Humor* (Portage, Mich.: Fellowship of Merry Christians, 1996), 36.
3. See Romans 12:6–8, 11; 1 Corinthians 15:58; Hebrews 6:10–12; 2 Peter 1:5–11.
4. See Matthew 24:45–46; 25:21, 23; 1 Corinthians 4:2; Revelation 2:10.
5. See Matthew 22:39; Romans 12:10; 13:8; 1 Corinthians 16:14; Galatians 5:14, 22; 1 Thessalonians 4:9.
6. Dallas Willard, "Spiritual Formation in Christ for the Whole Life and the Whole Person," *Vocatio* 12.2 (spring 2001): 6.

Chapter 2: When You've Done Your Best

1. For parallel accounts see Matthew 26:6–13 and John 12:1–8.
2. "You are the light of the world. A city on a hill cannot be hidden. Neither do people light a lamp and put it under a bowl. Instead they put it on its stand, and it gives light to everyone in the house. In the same way, let your light shine before men, that they may see your good deeds and

praise your Father in heaven" (Matt. 5:14–16). If our good deeds cause others to praise God (whether now or later, in time or eternity), then all good deeds are for Him, because ultimately all good deeds glorify Him.

3. William McRae, *The Dynamics of Spiritual Gifts* (Grand Rapids: Zondervan, 1976), 54; cited in *Christianity Today* 18.13 (29 March 1974): 39.

4. Names and details of this account have been changed.

5. "The Dick Staub Interview: James Lee Burke Is a Cowboy with a Conscience." At *christianitytoday.com/ct/2004/126/33.0* (6/30/2004).

6. *Bits and Pieces,* June 1990, 13. Quoted in *10,000 Sermon Illustrations* (Dallas: Biblical Studies Press, 2000).

Chapter 3: When God Doesn't Defend

1. *Signs of the Times,* March 1988, 12. Quoted in *10,000 Sermon Illustrations* (Dallas, Tex.: Biblical Studies Press), 2000.

2. Ibid.

3. Ibid.

4. A. W. Tozer, *The Knowledge of the Holy* (New York: Harper and Row, 1961), 62.

5. Ibid., 63.

6. J. I. Packer, *Knowing God* (Downers Grove, Ill.: InterVarsity, 1993), 80.

7. Tozer, *Knowledge of the Holy,* 115.

Chapter 4: When Your Critic Speaks the Truth

1. Don Phillips, *Washington Post,* 6 July 2000, Internet Edition. At www.washingtonpost.com.

2. Ibid.

Chapter 5: When to Blow It Off

1. Bernie May, Wycliffe Bible Translators newsletter, July 1983.

2. Edythe Draper, *Draper's Book of Quotations for the Christian World* (Wheaton, Ill.: Tyndale House, 1992), 3848.

Chapter 6: When to Take a Stand

1. Edythe Draper, *Draper's Book of Quotations for the Christian World* (Wheaton, Ill.: Tyndale House, 1992), 2071.

Chapter 8: When Primed to Fire

1. *The Far Side Desk Calendar,* 1998 (©FarWorks, Inc.; Kansas City: Andrews McMeel, 1997), 15 January.

2. Oswald Chambers, quoted in *Bible Illustrator,* CD-ROM, version 3 (Parson's Technology), index 2296–2301.

3. Author unknown; cited in Michael P. Green, *Illustrations for Biblical Preaching,* CD-ROM (Grand Rapids: Baker, 1989).

Chapter 9: When an Explosion Seems Inevitable

1. Quoted at GCFL.net: The Good, Clean Funnies List; Harvest, Ala.
2. Ibid.
3. See Acts 11:5–17. This text is likely a summary of Peter's presentation.
4. An adaptation from James S. Hewett, *Illustrations Unlimited* (Wheaton, Ill.: Tyndale House, 1988), 332.
5. Quoted in Lewis H. Lapham, "Tremendous Trifles: Political Campaigning," *Harper's*, August 1999.
6. "Incentive Awards: The Changing Face of Performance Recognition" (Dallas: U.S. Office of Personnel Management, 2000), 1.

Chapter 10: When You Don't Want to Forgive

1. *Reader's Digest*, July 1995, 16.
2. Edythe Draper, *Draper's Book of Quotations for the Christian World* (Wheaton, Ill.: Tyndale House, 1992), 4104.
3. Quoted at bpfrommer.com/God~Grant~Me~The~Senility.